***

"Black life is a carnival and a sanctuary, showcasing our journeys with joy and pain through eras of blood-stained glass..."
-Dennis Maurice

Copyright © 2021
Very Black Books
veryBlackbooks.com
info@veryBlackbooks.com

All rights reserved.
ISBN-13: 978-0-578-86619-2

BLACK WASHED

A Collection of Essays, Poems, Dreams, and Letters Addressed to Black Folk

Dennis Maurice Dumpson

Foreword Curated by: Black Women

(Melonee D. Gaines; Joy V. Harris; Ivory Allison; Dreena Whitfield-Brown; Gloria McNeil; Stephanie D. Keene; TheeAmazingGrace (Gracie Berry); Leonia Johnson; Paula Ogden-Artwell; Adrianne S. Dumpson-Diggs)

BLACK WASHED
Collection of Essays, Poems, Dreams, and Letters Addressed to Black Folk

BY CHAPTERS

I   The Mercy Seat | 1

II   Nobody Sleep | 22

III   Black & Empty | 36

IV   Between Hands & Clay | 52

V   Everything Will Burn | 63

VI   Lynching Language | 78

VII   Rest Without Compromise | 96

VIII   Black as Cain | 107

IX   Deeply Hood | 117

X   Halos & Headwraps | 129

contents

ADDRESSED TO BLACK FOLK

v about the cover
vii dedication
ix memoriam & honor
xviii introduction: black lemons
xxi about the foreword

10	The Sit In
13	He Ain't Heavy
19	The Back of the Spoon
30	Something to Cry About
33	G.R.I.T.S.
41	Body Heat
44	All Fourths Matter
49	Decolonizing Romance

BLACK WASHED
Collection of Essays, Poems, Dreams, and Letters Addressed to Black Folk

contents

ADDRESSED TO BLACK FOLK

58	For These Porcelain Harbors
61	Resting My Eyes
71	Bad Lighting
74	Everything Will Burn
76	Church Punch
87	Vertigo
90	Lynching Language
93	Black Lemons

contents

ADDRESSED TO BLACK FOLK

102	Requiem
104	No Bone
112	A 3-Tier Cake
114	Black & Empty
125	Carnal Hymns
127	Deeply Hood
135	How Is Sugar Born?
138	Optics & Capital
142	Alive In This Skin

The Fastening (Epilogue)
144

BLACK WASHED
A Collection of Essays, Poems, Dreams, and Letters Addressed to Black Folk

Acknowledgements

About the
Cover Design

Design: Jameil Johnson | @mealy.jpg
Optics: Darryl Cobb, Jr. | @darrylcobb

It is not about what you did; it is about *how* you did it. It's about Jameil using the shades and hues of the cover muses' skin to create the authentic, melanin rich gradient used for addressing the foreword's label on the cover. It's about Darryl giving folk so much confidence that each muse looks like freedom & poetry bathed in joy and good lighting. I see you as more than creatives. You are liberating our identities by capturing our fullness and I love y'all for lending your passions and talents. Thank you.

About the
Cover Muses

(Vaneeda; Jason; Dylan; Adrianne; Devin; Tiffany†; Joy; Chatara; Inga; Stephen; Tyson; Terica; Danielle; Janine; April; Yasmin; Jennifer; Sherneen; Dennis; Angela; Tanesha; Emily; Rhonda; Ivory; Jamilah; Alanna; Lauren; Shonda; Keeya; and Gracie)

There are about 328 million people in America, and we all share approximately 5,200 first names. This means that on average about 63,000 people walk around with the same name. Yet somehow, I was able to convene more than 30 friends from Philly, Baltimore, Indiana, D.C., Jersey, South Carolina; California; and Uganda without a single overlap in name. It may seem small, but to me it resembles the exceptionally gorgeous feelings I have for each of you. Surely, there are folk who may resemble you, but in the confines of rooms we share and the space we make for each other there is only one you—and it is my honor to have each you as part of this ensemble of rare Black beauty. Thank you so much for bringing your energy and soul glow to this cover and, most importantly, to my life. We photographed this as my 34th birthday gift with an intention to wash the cover with brilliant, beautiful Black folk. I will always remember your generosity. Thank you. I love you all.

BLACK WASHED
A Collection of Essays, Poems, Dreams, and Letters Addressed to Black Folk

Dedicated to
My Mother

This book is dedicated to the most reliable love in my life.
This book is dedicated to the steady beat in my heart.
This book is dedicated to the enthusiastic drum, humbly beating throughout my song.
This book is dedicated to the sturdiest brick in my house.
This book is dedicated to the strongest rock God lent me in this weary land.

This book is dedicated to My Mommy.

Thank you for recognizing, inspiring, and putting up with my anointing.
Thank you for advocating for my destiny.
Thank you for securing space for my dreams in your prayers.

You are living water and I am hydrated by each sermon you speak over my life. I will always be grateful and honored that you make the conscious effort to love me more powerfully than I merit.

Thank you for stowing my baggage on your back, so I can fly free.
Thank you for wrapping my gifts and opening them for me.
Thank you for opening a bank of love and letting me withdrawal when I had no deposit.

I will never be able to pay you back, but I will always try. This entire book is dedicated to you.

All my love… Always my love… All ways I love you,

Denny

Acknowledgements

My Mother, Adrianne (2017) | Photography Credit: Alex Moorer

BLACK WASHED
A Collection of Essays, Poems, Dreams, and Letters Addressed to Black Folk

In Memoriam

Since publishing my first book, *What My Colored Eyes See: The Words of a Decorated Child*, in 2009 many of my strongest supporters have become my most diligent ancestors. I love them with deep, untamed passion. My previous book was dedicated in the honor and memory of my grandmother, Lucile Dumpson, and since that time many others have joined her in victory. While there are many that can be named and have the right to be celebrated, as we begin this collection, I am remembering three family members and one friend who contributed to my life and believe in me with deep love.

I pray all our ancestors, seated in glory, are resting without compromise. I love you all.

Acknowledgements

In Memoriam
Carolyn Richardson ✝

September 27, 1947 – May 25, 2013

    My aunt Carolyn was a creative and energetic spirit with equal parts compassion and fire. My earliest memories of her, are creating set designs, stacking wigs for church plays, preparing us to speak for a special occasion during service, and making sure all the children (who are now close to or over 40) were seen and heard. There are so many memories of her, like driving in her Benz after watch night service (if you know, you know). She wanted to make church fun and she always centered youthful exploration in her teaching of God. One day she called me, and we were chatting it up, and I asked her if she needed anything specific and she said, "Well I needed to talk to you that's why I called…" (no request, just me). She broke down the wall of transactional love and her interactions with you were so meaningful, because of their intimacy and that familiarity became the necessity. She is still one of the realest in my book and I love her deep in the same ways she poured love all over me. Her and my grandma (her big sister) passed away on the same day, nine years apart, in the same hour—during day and night, respectively—so I know she was welcomed into the Kingdom of Glory, lauded in love. She decorates so many of my memories today, just like she did when she was here physically. I miss you and will always love you, Aunt Carolyn. Rest in Love.

BLACK WASHED
A Collection of Essays, Poems, Dreams, and Letters Addressed to Black Folk

In Memoriam

May 15, 1933 – September 2, 2016

Aunt Ro, Ro-Ro, Aunt Rosa, Matriarch, Deaconess, Sister, Mother, Grandmother are all earthly synonyms for Rosa Lee Johnson. Aunt Ro was the first person to lift you up when you needed. She believed in the Lord and what she knew he was going to do and if you spent just a little time with her you were bound to believe in His promise of benedictions, too. She reveled in opportunities to be good to folk. Her life was defined by sweet, unconditional care for her family, friends, church, community, and even strangers. She was a teacher, by profession, and always had a word waiting for you. The way she left this life was so profound. Aunt Ro was determined to host the fish fry for our family reunion, but as you can imagine folk were concerned about our 80+ year old matriarch planning an event for 100 people. However, what she told you she was going to do, she did. She pressed on with her children and planned a big to-do for all of us. Everyone celebrated and she sat on the red bench outside her home the entire day reveling in the joy of good care. The last guest left and Aunt Ro, seated on the red bench in front of her earthly home, went to her eternal home just like that. This is poetry. I love you more than words can express. Everything is different since you left, but our love will remain unchanged. Rest well, Aunt Ro.

Acknowledgements

In Memoriam
James Howard Dumpson †

March 8, 1937 – February 3, 2018

Pop-Pop. My grandfather was a baker for close to 40 years. He worked at a Jewish bakery located in, what is now popularized as, the Northern Liberties section of Philadelphia. He would leave for work before dawn and walk or catch the bus to his job most times, six days per week. He used his hands to mix, to lift, to knead, and to mold bread and never complained once about his job.

If I have any regret about our relationship it is that I did not realize he was such a good listener and an active educator. Unlike many teachers who refer to curriculum and assert their knowledge of subject matter, my Pop-Pop was a teacher that made you feel like the expert. I went to South America for a residency capstone while in business school and Pop-Pop was excited. He gave me a couple proud smiles as we talked leading up to my departure and he listened to everything I expected to do and learn while I was there.

When I saw him, just shy of a month later, he had questions. And he was specific. "Denny, I looked up BRF they're a pretty cool company." "Aramark is making it good for shareholders, so that must mean the little guy is in the toilet!" "Tell me what you know about shareholder value." He researched everything I told him—without a computer or smart phone, only his Wall Street Journal and Forbes, I am sure.

BLACK WASHED
A Collection of Essays, Poems, Dreams, and Letters Addressed to Black Folk

When I went to share what I thought were the more exciting aspects of my trip—my visit to the Andes or travel through Brazil—he quickly redirected me to what I said I wanted to learn before I left, and he positioned me as an expert and scholar.

Pop-Pop saw no value in me being subservient to him or his love, instead he proudly acted like I could teach him something (he was a self-taught business and finance scholar in his own right). His manner just seemed like Pop-Pop being Pop-Pop, but as I look back, I recognize that he loved me so much that he made room for me shine and show up. That is a good teacher. I wish I could acknowledge it when he was alive, but I am so glad to have that as a reminder as I live. Pop-Pop, I could fill up this entire book expressing my love, admiration, and joy of knowing your type of love.

Memories are flooding! Even as I look at your memoriam photo here, as you were offering your interview for Mommy's 50th *Slay Day* (that means birthday) documentary and I asked you to say, "Happy 50th Slay Day, Adrianne!" And you said, "What is this medieval time, slay means to kill! Why would want me to say a thing like that about my daughter?!" Followed by your signature and comical grunt of disgust at my antics. You were never absent from the joke; you were in on it and many times leading it. More substantively, I remember when I told you I was gay, and you said "Well, OK, Denny, people like all types of things these days." Even when it did not seem like it, you made it easy to be me. I will never forget how you pushed me to expand my territory and life, unconditionally. Every decision I made or move I was considering your position was to push me closer to my confidence and I am so thankful for you.

I love you, Pop-Pop. I hope grandma knows how hard you worked to fulfill the responsibilities she left with you before she passed. I was blessed to have spent time with you and hold your hand as you transitioned from this life to the next. I was one of your children and you are my *sun*.
Rest well, Pop-Pop.

Photography Credit: Dwight Moore-Green

Acknowledgements

In Memoriam
Tiffany Gilbert †

September 12, 1982 – February 14, 2021

Weeks before publishing *Black Washed*, one of my good friends, who is featured on the printed cover and whom I have known for 24 years, Tiffany Gilbert, passed away. Her light was captivating, and her spirit was unquestionably magical. She supported everything I chose to do and cheered me on with her abundant and passionate love. She was a five-time cancer warrior, and you would never know it because it did not define how she expanded her life. Since high school I have always seen her as a beacon and I am so glad we deepened our relationship as adults at house parties, celebrating birthdays, drinking prosecco on rooftops, loving on Black folk, and being #IDKBs. Tiffany, I will miss you forever and thank God for providing through you. I purposely chose this photo of you in the middle of a good laugh, because we were always in the middle of celebrating, laughing, and thinking about what's next! And we always will be.
Rest well, Tiff. I love you.

Photography Credit: Darryl Cobb, Jr

BLACK WASHED
A Collection of Essays, Poems, Dreams, and Letters Addressed to Black Folk

Honoring *Ancestors*

I believe, firmly, that we are lifted by ancestors.
I believe, firmly, that they carry us by our shirt collars when our feet get tired.
I believe, firmly, that when we think about giving up, they pinch our lips in the back of the sanctuary of our fears until we remember who we are.
I believe, firmly, that they hold our necks erect like monuments built from Obsidian.
I believe, firmly, that they glide into every room before we arrive and prepare it for us.
I believe, firmly, in the power of Black ancestors and recite some of their names as I begin this book:

Rebecca 'Shug' Montgomery, Elsie Stringfield,
Sally Scott, Lucile Dumpson,
Dr. James R. Dumpson, Carolyn Richardson,
Rosa Lee Johnson, James H. Dumpson, John Shaw,
Ernestene Richardson, Debra "Ann" Richardson-Bryant

… and a host of others that knew me before I knew myself.
I believe, feel, and love you, firmly. Thank you.

Acknowledgements

BLACK WASHED
A Collection of Essays, Poems, Dreams, and Letters Addressed to Black Folk

A Special
Thank You to...

Mom, Aunt Doris, Dev, Dyl, Inga, Rob, Joy, Ivory, Dreena, Alanna, Melonee, Emily, Fatima, Mealy, Chatara, and all the foreword authors, for sharing community with me and pushing me through the hurdles of creating *Black Washed*. You extended grace in the many ways you have honored our fight to complete this collection of thoughts. You encouraged so much that is illuminated on these pages.
I will never forget your brilliant love.

I love you.

Introduction: *Black Lemons*

BLACK WASHED
A Collection of Essays, Poems, Dreams, and Letters Addressed to Black Folk

I love to cook. If I were not writing this, I imagine I would be a restauranteur, or chef. I often research the origins of global spices used in cuisine. That is how I learned about black lemons.

Black lemons are, in fact, limes that have been dehydrated, looted of their juice, oil, zest, and moisture until they are hardened on the inside and the out. Those limes, once dried out, are grated as an essential spice to add a uniquely vibrant flavor to otherwise mundane cuisine. The flavor is said to be sweet and acidic, with a taste that has no known substitute. Generally, when I learn of a new culturally profound spice, I am excited, and I want to use it in a dish immediately. However, this time I questioned why black lemons had to grow up this way. The story of the black lemon felt like kin and my reaction was soaked with intimacy.

The heritage of Black folk and Black life are often—and, in my opinion, too frequently—shrunk by our energetic story of being killed, yet never dying. We are the lead actors in nonfiction stories about the immorality of captivity, capitalism, and colonization instead of those perverted enough to commit and continue the acts. Like black lemons, Black folk had juice, and oil, and zest, and moisture before all the attempts to kill our fruits. That is our story; too seldom told. The usefulness of black lemons' uniquely sweet and sharp flavor, that cannot be duplicated, is most certainly valuable. Yet to wait for any living thing to dry and die before acknowledging its value is obscene, crooked, and depraved.

As I wrote *Black Washed*, I went through various changes in how I presented content. As I see it, much of the optics of Blackness treats Black folk like the black lemons—only useful to the narrative after we have been exhausted, dried, grated down, and dead. In much of the public sphere, especially those curated for white eyes and those who value white things, Black life has been codified to exist in stages that begin with our death or fight to live. Making the essence, the juice, the oil, the zest, the moisture in Black life an allegory that exists in some place alien to Black folk.

I finished writing *Black Washed* four times. I have been announcing its arrival for about four years. While I wish I would not have shared such a lengthy promotional period, I am so glad I waited before I published. Much of its earlier penning centered us as black lemons with limited to no acknowledgement for our beautiful Black lives. This was not my intention, yet it was a symptom of how constructed narratives and white terror influence my understandings of us and me.

What you are preparing to read is a collection of thoughts and opining and writing and ideas and emotions spanning the past decade—curated to celebrate Blackness, Black life, and Black folk with the respect we are due. Our stories are not the various ways we have been killed, abused, oppressed, and maligned, solely. Our stories are also how we swaddled ourselves in Black life before we knew it was being attacked. We are fresh limes and black lemons, and while both are valuable, for far too long, our juice, our oil, our zest, and our moisture have not led the conversation.

Introduction | Black Lemons

We are greater than a world held hostage. As a Black writer my job is to reveal truth and evidence. To me, *Black Washed* proves that the existence of Black lives is the best ontological argument that there is a God and devils. The value of Black lives cannot be bastardized as the spice grated into this trite stew of invented myths. Black life does not begin when the systems and practices of this world wear us down. We were a juicy, oily, zesty, well moisturized collection of somebodies before terror and pain. In this, I am contributing my celebration of Black life to our literary canon.

I have been—and still am—scared that I will shift to *the other side of soil* without making a profound, unbending impact. I know the pressure and longing to empty every bit of yourself, so you can return it to the world and all its supervising deities. I know the terror of pushing myself to my ends, because the idea of leaving with my gifts unopened feels disgusting, irresponsible, and ugly.

Everything I do… Everything I write… Everything I produce… Everything is symptomatic of my personal fight against the anxiety of not opening every gift inside of me and give them all away. My fear of not leaving this earth empty is a loneliness that I cannot adequately explain, yet that panic pushed me to publish *Black Washed*.

Toni Morrison once shared that James Baldwin mentioned that Black writers are often fighting against the little white man on our shoulders—all up in our business, telling us to not go that far, and controlling our truths. More than a half-century later and I am still beating that same little white man's ass; trying to evict him from my home. It is hard. My life has long been invaded by whiteness and its sensibilities and over time I have, regrettably, adopted many of them as my own.

Rehabilitating my mind to not believe in these constructs, that are fictional yet sturdy, has been a journey. It is still work. Through this collection I hope my personal journeys offer confidence for the broader Black body in reconciling the ways we honor and dishonor Black life to outlast the snares, terror, and treacheries of this world. I am demanding the eviction of shame from the lungs of breathing Black bodies in breathing Black worlds.

My greatest hope is that what we have compiled in this collection speaks to Black folk with decency and respect and honors our anointing. Black life is a carnival and a sanctuary showcasing our journeys with joy and pain through eras of blood-stained glass. And that alone is worthy of celebrations.

Welcome.

BLACK WASHED
A Collection of Essays, Poems, Dreams, and Letters Addressed to Black Folk

Black Women
FOREWORD AUTHORS

I	Melonee D. Gaines	2
II	Joy V. Harris	23
III	Ivory Allison	37
IV	Dreena Whitfield-Brown	53
V	Gloria McNeil	64
VI	Stephanie D. Keene	79
VII	TheeAmazingGrace (Gracie Berry)	97
VIII	Leonia Johnson	108
IX	Paula Ogden-Artwell	118
X	Adrianne Dumpson-Diggs	130

About the Foreword Authors

Some people are fans of actors, I am a fan of activists.
Many of my favorite activists are Black women. Initially when I began writing content for this book in 2008, I planned to honor Black women through my words. I was determined to celebrate their genius, their activism, their steadfastness, their prayerful existence. I spent a decade expressing my love and admiration for Black women and I was incredibly unimpressed with myself.

Frustrated and, frankly, tired of my on-again off-again romance with the celebration I created for Black women, I sat in prayer for an answer. I did not get one immediately, but I recognized the festivity was too expensive to produce and I was unable to pay the cost to speak on their behalf.

Some people are fans of actors, I am a fan of activists.
On January 18, 2018, my good friend—and Black woman foreword author— Dreena, got me and my friend, Ivory, passes to see her client, Patrisse Cullors, abolitionist and co-founder of the Black Lives Matter movement, and asha bandele, former features editor at <u>Essence Magazine</u> and author (*The Prisoner's Wife*; *Daughter*), present their new co-authored book, *When They Call You A Terrorist: A Black Lives Matter Memoir*. I met Patrisse and asha backstage, which was amazing, because I am a fan of activists.

They ended their thrilling conversation, moderated by professor and luminary, Dr. Marc Lamont Hill, and introduced through the poetry of Miriam Harris (Jawn the Baptist), in the overflowing Free Library of Philadelphia auditorium. They began reading pre-written questions that begged for Patrisse and asha's guidance. One of the questions {paraphrased} read, 'The Black Lives Matter movement receives lots of criticism about it not having visible leadership. Do you think that will potentially stunt its growth? How do you respond to the critique that this is a leaderless movement?'* Patrisse prefaced her response with exceedingly kind remarks for the question and an acknowledgement that this was not the first time she has

BLACK WASHED
A Collection of Essays, Poems, Dreams, and Letters Addressed to Black Folk

heard that critique. However, it is what she said next that shook me up and turned me around. She said {paraphrased}, '…However, BLM is not a leaderless movement. You actually came here today to see me, a visible leader in the movement, and I wrestle with the question, because I believe when people say we are leaderless they actually mean that we are not the Black, cis-gendered male orators or preachers that they're used to—but we are here.'*

I could not sit still—there was no rest—the remainder of my time in their presence and I could not wait to go outside in the cold with my friend—and Black woman foreword author—Ivory to soberly bear witness. It was at that point that I recognized that I had no business spending any time trying to curate language and platitudes on the behalf of Black women. They have their own voice, their own language, and the agency to speak up for themselves. It was on this day that I gave a call to my mother, Stephanie, Dreena, Gracie, Joy, and Melonee and told them what I learned before asking them to write the foreword for *Black Washed*.

As you journey through 10 chapters in this book, you will read their responses to this:

> *In the form of an essay, poem, dream, or letter: If you were to teach the world how to properly wash Black women what would be your lesson?"*

When you begin a new chapter in this book you will be greeted by the beauty a Black woman has curated through her elegant response. I am acutely aware and embarrassed at how easy it was for me to forget that Black women have voice, agency, and clarity over their own experiences. No one else can speak on their behalf and I am thankful for each of them offering their voices and celebration to this collection. Each foreword author is a dear sister or mother of mine and, as Black women often do, they have each been a stone fortress for my deepest hopes and dreams.

To Black women and our foreword authors: Some people are fans of actors, I am a fan of activists and there are no better champions for humanity than Black women. You have lifted Black men, Black children, Black culture, Black history, Black futures, and yourselves with grace and righteousness. I am honored to share space with you here and everywhere else we will travel. Thank you for enriching the content and intentionality of this communion among Black folk. I am not centering your stories; your stories are central. While we do not deserve you, your stories deserve to be showcased with care. I hope you feel honored by this body of work. I am a fan. I love you all.

*Retrieved from the author's notes during the event.

About the Foreword Authors

Foreword Authors
(L to R: Leonia; Joy; Stephanie; Gloria; Adrianne; Paula)
Photography Credit: Darryl Cobb, Jr.

BLACK WASHED
A Collection of Essays, Poems, Dreams, and Letters Addressed to Black Folk

Foreword Authors
(Top L to Bottom R: Ivory; TheeAmazingGrace (Gracie); Melonee; Dreena)
Photography Credit (Ivory): Meredith Edlow

DENNIS MAURICE

THE MERCY SEAT *One*

"Why this church had such a hateful vendetta against cake and punch was beyond me.

I saw my Aunt Rosa making coconut cake yesterday and I picked up the can of pineapple she stewed down into a jam to fill the center. So, I knew what time it was. Retta and I shared mixing blades from the bowl, and it was scrumptious before cooked—these folk don't understand what they are missing. I only came here for the cake and punch of it all—although church was non-negotiable.

Now Rev. Stephens is yelling from the pulpit; "You best find your way to *the Mercy Seat*. Get right with God and do it now!" I was not quite sure what this seat was, but I knew it had to be my rite of passage before I could have my slice and my guzzle, so here I sit. We listen to the preacher, we eat cake, and all the kids reenact what we saw during service—that was church to me. Eventually, Ms. Porter caught the Holy Ghost, and another, and another. Once they were *caught up in the spirit*, they would send them to the dining room for punch and cake while they got themselves together. They better be glad I don't know how to catch this Holy Ghost yet, or I'd be buckin' and fussin', too! Folk were *"cutting the monkey"* as mom-mom would say, so service was ending. "If his next words ain't, 'May the Lord watch between me and thee…' I might snap!"

I was good & grown before I understood ritual and invitation. I wrote this when I was 20 years old.

Being invited to rest on mercy, lay down burdens, revel in a new song, and understand it better by and by is an extravagant gift almost as sweet as coconut cake and punch.

Welcome to Chapter one: The Mercy Seat—Foreword Author: Melonee D. Gaines.

BLACK WASHED | *A Collection of Essays, Poems, Dreams, and Letters Addressed to Black Folk*

One

Foreword Author

Melonee D. Gaines

Melonee D. Gaines is the owner and lead maven of MPact Media Group, a media and public relations consulting firm. She has written for MLK50.com, WKNO News, High Ground News, *Edible Memphis*, *CRISIS Magazine*, and TheGrio.com. She also works as a literacy specialist with Shelby County Schools and has taught from pre-K to higher education for more than 15 years.

Her career has included programming and public relations work with the Southern University of New Orleans, the American Black Film Festival, and Essence Festival, and educational outreach and fundraising alongside communities in Baltimore, Atlantic City, Detroit, Flint, and rural Mississippi.

Born by the water in New Orleans and rooted on her grandmother's land in Picayune, Mississippi, Melonee has made Memphis her home for the last 10 years. She holds degrees in English literature from the University of Southern Mississippi and the University of Memphis. She is the proud mother to a teenage womanist-in-training and a happy shih tzu. A professed oxtail enthusiast, a devout traveler, and a music lover, you can follow her intellectual reverie on Twitter @melohello.

BLACK WASHED | *A Collection of Essays, Poems, Dreams, and Letters Addressed to Black Folk*

My Sacrifice and Alms in the Temple of Black Women

Melonee D. Gaines

DENNIS MAURICE

> Aaaaayeee babo.
> I spit on the ground
> I spit language on the dust
> I spit memory on the water
> I spit hope on this seminary
> I spit teeth on the wonder of women, holy volcanic women
> Recapturing the memory of our most sacred sounds.
>
> -From "Aaaaayeee Babo" by Sonia Sanchez

Before I knew it, my mother was out of her chair and screaming and jumping—a belly full of rage, sorrow, and tears flooded the pew. I was only eight at the time I saw my mother go into the Holy Ghost. It was scary and inspiring, a type of rite of passage I thought all adults eventually go through. One day, I thought, I will experience this. This is what makes God real.

I remember looking over and being still because it was the first-time, I had ever seen my mother take flight. For too many years, I had seen her beaten by my father and watched her sanguinary will flood and splash the floor and walls. But this time, I saw her in full glory. Powerful!

"Ahhhhhh! Thank you, God! Thank you, father!" She jumped and reached for the sky. She clapped her hands. She hollered out in a way that should have embarrassed me, but even at that age, I knew God was at work.

One by one, women in white came over to my mother. One held her back as my mother jumped and flailed. Another joined and began to cool my mother with the white Jesus fan with the advert for Brown's Funeral Home on the back. Another came and stood in front of her and began praying over her until she sat. A final woman came and began to rub her back and wipe her brow. Eventually, my mother lay prostrate on the pew.

I knew all these women in white—matrons of our community and names appended with Mae or Jean. Or sometimes, they would call each other by their last name—"Hey there, Lee!" when they strolled past the house. As I grew up, I learned pieces of the stories of the women in white and how they survived childhood sexual abuse, incest, abandonment, abusive or philandering husbands, and sharecropping. These were women that would stop by our house and sit with my mother and drink coffee and eat tea cakes in the kitchen for what seemed like hours. I had learned to play silently and not listen to their conversations when these women in white would come over.

God is a woman, and she loves her coffee Black. No sugar. No cream.

BLACK WASHED | *A Collection of Essays, Poems, Dreams, and Letters Addressed to Black Folk*

Sometimes, the women in white would come over and stand at the fence line to receive portions of the harvest from our garden. I wondered if they knew what horror we were living under. That my quiet stares were calls for help. If they saw the welts on my mother's body. If they knew that someday my mother may not be here.

Somehow, my mother, my dear Aquarian mother, lived. She lived to tell me her story. In pieces. In time.

Come. Celebrate our footsteps insatiable as sudden breathing
Love curves the journey to these women sails
Love says Awoman. Awoman to these tongues of thunder

-From "Aaaaayeee Babo" by Sonia Sanchez

I waded in the waters as far from the shore as I could get and until the current barely lifted my feet from the ocean floor—the water lapping the seam of my lips. The ocean kissed and carried the stream of my tears. Afloat in my sorrow, I fixed my eyes onto the blue line in the red sky. I knew love was around me. Thank you, Sonia. I was remembering a love that now lay dying before me. It was the moment I decided to leave my husband.

It was a love that cocooned the inner child, trapping her inside with her wounds.

It was a love that required heat to burrow in my skin, down into my bones.

It was a love that needed to mourn the loss of my old shell.

It was a love that raged about because it was not seen.

It was a love that could not be.

I became a woman.

I am a new kind of love that listens to the water.

It is a love that looks to the color of the sky for a reckoning.

It is a love that moved past the weariness of a long-held sorrow that shucked about and laid waste to my creation.

It is a love that knew my Mama loved me and I ladled her best parts into my womb.

It is a love that had to forgive and soothe the wounds of a past filled with sunsets.

DENNIS MAURICE

It is a love that held on to the memory of my father singing to me, giving me the one song that pulled me out of my heartbreak.

> Gonna find a few, who will always walk with you
> oh baby - many people claim, but their view's the same
>
> What I wanna do, and what I'd like to tell you
> may not be, as you see,
> as you live today, what I wanna say
> Is be ever wonderful in your own sweet way

It is a love story and I survived to tell it. In pieces. In time. To my daughter while she is young. Awoman.

> Come praise our innocence
> our decision to be human
> reenter the spirit of morning doves
> and our God is near
> I say our God is near
> I say our God is near
> Aaaayeee babo Aaaayeee babo Aaaayeee babo
> (Praise God).
>
> -From "Aaaaayeee Babo" by Sonia Sanchez

We haven't manifested the love we desire until we are washed in the celebration of our survival. Until then, I decided to run. I ran from confrontation. I ran from my voice. I ran from my marriage. I called it living in my head. I called it introverted silence. I called it solitude. I was running all by myself and nobody was chasing me. I made it impossible for anyone to catch me. I saved face by wearing a mask. I was the strong friend. I was the independent, angry Black woman.

I was tired. I became weary. I was alone. I became lonely.

I was chasing shadows to hide in. I did not want to recognize the humanity of my wounds.

I was in this life because I chose it. The truth of those words washed over me.

The one truth that gave me grace were the friends I chose as family. My life created a sanctuary where friends became family as a necessity for my survival. After years under fire, my family fled to safe spaces and peered out nervously. I dared the world to see me, yet my wounds kept me bound to an infirmary of solitude.

God, I thank you. To be washed in a friend's prayer…to know that God saw fit to send people in my life to cover me. In my imperfection, I managed to know what love is but did not trust myself with it in my hands. What could my love do? I was drifting through life with blinders on not realizing the world I was building around me was beautiful. My blinders only projected a battlefield before me.

As I went colliding through my divorce, I looked to friends who witnessed me endure the pain of it all. I had to form new traditions for holidays, new ways to celebrate a life worthy of my living and intentions.

I remember dear sister friends welcoming me to their home in Baltimore and taking me to a Korean bath house. It was the first time I had to strip away all that confined me in this world to really see myself. Naked in a room full of women, I washed my body timidly but with *a knowing* that I needed to purify all that was lost in me and hand it over to God. Those things had served me well. Fear. Anger. Depression. Worry. Anxiety.

I remember seeing the swirling pools of water. Women of different hues walking around indifferent to the nakedness, the scars, the blemishes, the stretch marks, the story of every other woman's body in the sanctuary. As I showered, I watched one woman crouched to the floor with an ecru bowl of steaming water. She poured it slowly over her head, chest, back. Her body moved smoothly as the water set a course down her body and to the floor. The woman next to her set to work on her own body rubbing a soapy emollient over her arms slowly. She brought the mixture to the tips of her fingers and seemed to wiggle them a bit when she reached the end—casting out spells and scabs against her womanhood. At that moment, I let go and became fully aware that my body had nothing, absolutely nothing to apologize for. Every decision I had been making for myself was serving my soul's work.

As I entered the clement pool of water, I looked over to my sister friends with gratitude in my soul. I remember great periods of silence mixed with laughter. They checked in on me.

Are you good? You straight?

I don't remember crying that day. Maybe I did. But the sweetness of the heat and sweat of the bathhouse was the recuperation of my divine feminine consciousness.

I thank my sister friends because I had to leave behind the fear of being vulnerable in front of those who love me to my bare bones.

I had been hurt, wounded by the end of my love story, but there was a fear in knowing that I was strong. My love is as strong and as enduring as the connections I have formed. *Repeat that.*

DENNIS MAURICE

God is a woman and she makes women with spines of palm and hearts of lazulum.

Our love requires the breadth of our words and as *a woman*, we must lift the buoyant fevers of our soul's inferno to light the way. This pussy is the continuum of empires, legacies, juju, and goulash that spoon-fed those who endured to love me wholly. Our friends are made in our image. Realize this: our hands carved this land and scooped this sea. What of this life will you make it?

I found myself adrift in that ocean, feeling like I had bottomed out of love. My tears meeting the water goddess in me, around me, through me, I knew my love had kept me afloat. It had kept me alive. It made me want to rejoice. My Holy Ghost suspended in the current.

What words could I spit forth and praise God? My mother gave God her gratitude. I give God the celebration of my words. I will sow them into the world I create.

Bring the stool of your sorrow at the base of the waterfall but be ready to rise and sing at the altar call of love.

God is a woman and she gives us water when the sky does not fall.

BLACK WASHED | *A Collection of Essays, Poems, Dreams, and Letters Addressed to Black Folk*

The Sit In

A Poem Addressed to Black Folk

The Sit In

I sit in two worlds:
Come Again?
and
Fukumean?
Conflicting tones. One message.

I sit in two worlds:
Come again, Paul? I think you've got me misunderstood.
and
Whachanahgondu is any of that, Pat.

No matter how I articulate it, you get where I am going and know it ain't looking good…
For you.

I sit in two worlds:
Let's agree to disagree, Nadine. I need to get ready for my 2:15.
and
I said what I said, Chrissy. Let me go on, 'cuz ya ass is tryin' me…

I sit in two worlds:
With multiple languages,
Didactic tongues,
Intentional phrases…
That host a sit in at your lunch counter, but they ain't come to eat.
And my chants were never for your appreciation—get ya ass out my Gahtdam seat.

I sit in two worlds:
One sits on the top
One lives underneath.
And I can only depend on my unswerving Black universe for relief.

I sit in two worlds:
Blessing these jokers with my multiplicity while venerating my ethnicity
Affirmatively reading you for all your toxicity

BLACK WASHED | *A Collection of Essays, Poems, Dreams, and Letters Addressed to Black Folk*

You can monitor my daily voyages and will never see me trip.
I am the conversation starter.
I got the juice; you want a sip.

I got my degree in the Black polyglot and now you're in my class.
Griots taught us an urbane language while learning how to reconcile lack.
You think you're eating creamy polenta? That's my Mama grits warming on the eye in back.
My earliest professors spoke with words they learned but ate with tongues they know.

Ancestors feed me from a brilliant gumbo pot, seasoned with global Black spices like it's Doro Wat.
They comfort my garment by patting its weave, adorned it with icy collars and bamboo earlobes.
Bodies sculpted from rock epochs have lain in the Nile, spiritually placed on the necks of Afrophiles.

This dual citizenship was not planned, but there is no curse.
I am guided by one universe—hugging every syllable, kissing every verse.
My ether is blessed with finesse like NAS' 215-bar rhyme.
My flow is angled perfectly, I am ready, and I got the time.

I may sit in two worlds, but of this world I am not.
I am sounds you cannot re-hear.
I am looks you thought you forgot.
I am the aroma of heavens with an unbreakable seal.
I am the genuine warmth you fashioned faux fur to feel.
You think you are feasting off the best part of my body, but you just chewin' on some peel.
(Read that twice)

I was created with worldly allure.
Black beats with bold, lurid, melodic tempos, using my locs to shatter chains on colonized door.
Incendiary,
I am the pin in the grenade…
and I'm the bomb.
I am the coffee, and I designed my own damn mug.
I may sit in two worlds, but in this universe, I am the plug.

DENNIS MAURICE

He Ain't Heavy

A Letter Addressed to my Black Brothers (Devin & Dylan)

BLACK WASHED | *A Collection of Essays, Poems, Dreams, and Letters Addressed to Black Folk*

He Ain't Heavy

October 2018

Dear Stoonks/Stinkapodahs (Dev & Dyl):

> "Black males who refuse categorization are rare, for the price of visibility in the contemporary world of white supremacy is that Black identity be defined in relation to the stereotype whether by embodying it or seeking to be other than it… Negative stereotypes about the nature of Black masculinity continue to overdetermine the identities Black males are allowed to fashion for themselves."
>
> – **bell hooks | We Real Cool: Black Men and Masculinity**

Imagine.

I woke up one morning and immediately fell into an unforgiving, sluggish cry for you.

Imagine.

The night before Mommy texted me while I was out at dinner. I opened the message, and it was Dyl's graduation photos. I had a fit. I could not control my energy. While I love you both deeply, this felt richer than any love I knew I had.

Imagine.

The next day I woke up with the relics of unresolved love and pain laying on top of me. I was hysterical. Flashbacks to memories of me resting on the carpet at 715, so that Dev could use my back to develop confidence in his crawling skills. Dev, you would crawl from my feet to my head and when you got to the top you would pull your chin over my forehead and lock upside-down eyes with me—as if you were making sure I knew you owned this mountain (also known as my back).

One day Inga asked me do I get tired of you crawling up and down my back and I said, "No he's not even that heavy…" I knew I had a responsibility to you, as so many others had a responsibility for my growth and care. I was never too heavy for them and you are never too heavy for me.

Imagine.

It is now 18 hours since I saw Dyl's graduation photos and I am still crying. No less arbitrary and no more understanding of the interior walls that were crumbling loudly in my two-bedroom apartment.

I started to think about Pop-Pop, who passed away this most recent winter, and the greatest gift he gave me—the gift of an imagination. He wanted me to dream big. He encouraged me to get fancy shoes, move away, get another degree, write a book, travel, and so much more. He did not push me, but he welcomed me into the idea that as a Black man I could have an imagination about my future that surpassed any relationship with his or my fear of it not being possible.

Imagine.

There is an unfair privilege and necessary consignment in being the eldest. The fact that I was born 10 and 18 years prior, respectively, signifies that I am part of the evidence that heritage, hope, and heroic living existed before you. I got to see the beauty of Black leadership and the strength in Black survival. I got to feel the warmth of our elders hugging without touch and loving you with no words.

And that is when it hit me. I was distraught, emotional, and socializing with my pain because the responsibility of being a back for you to crawl on, a strong arm to lift you, the carrier of romantic wisdom had finally grown from a choice to a calling. That concept is heavy…not you. The responsibility I feel for your success is heavy, but I must do my part to lift you up into manhood as best as I know.

Imagine.

Dyl, your heart is bright enough to light up the dimmest spaces and you will warm the iciest roads you travel with your love. I could use this letter to inform you of how vile the world you are contending with is, but I prefer spending this time informing you of how lit you are. Since the day mommy called me crying and frenzied—when I was in college and you were three years old—because you schooled yourself in unlocking doors and gave yourself permission to run out the house, I knew you were making space.

Imagine…

…unlocking those doors, again, today, Dyl. I want you to be fearless like the three-year-old that refused to wait for permission to run outside. I have always said you are too pure and beautiful and special for this world—we honestly do not deserve you, but we need you. You are like precious stone and essential and protective like bone. When you feel small, irrelevant, hesitant, or low I want you to **remember that your back is supported by a big brother that will never let you fall**, that respects the urgency of your rise, and believes in the joy of your success. You are a bold reflection of centuries of beautiful, Black legacy that lift you up. You are not here alone and when you feel like the only one, remember your gifts are rare and one-in-a-million. Your beautiful Black soul is your power source. Your beautiful Black soul is better than any diploma or degree. Your beautiful Black soul is your canvas, and you cannot paint the beautiful picture of your life without that foundation. Make some dope art in this life, Dyl.

Imagine.

Dev, when you laid on my back as a baby, I knew how energetic, connected, and empathic you were (and are). You believe in what you feel and as a Black man, that is also queer, like me, I know you will have lots of energy thrown your way. Be clear, Black folk will not always understand your manhood and other folk will misrepresent you from beneath their hoods. Yet, it is the complex magic you have inside that will draw you closer to the energy fit for you.

We were raised right—righter than most—and we have heritage and gifts in our joy that many will not recognize and will try to compromise. Own your destiny and never forget that the dynamisms you bring will be too much for some—that is fine. You should never linger any place you do not see God and that doesn't see the God in you.

Imagine…

…the beauty of only allowing energy as pure as yours anywhere near you, Brother. Imagine being so filled by your offering that you become the collection plate, Brother. Imagine celebrating that small child that climbed up backs in preparation for his ascension into a brilliant man that tells the mountains to turn to him, Brother.

Imagine first.

Brothers, this world does not have an imagination for Black folk, Black women, Black girls, Black families, Black queer folk, Black communities, Black lives, Black boys, or Black men. You must fashion yourself actively shouldering dreams in this life and know that I will back every one of your Black ass desires.

You have permission to build confidence while climbing my back.

Imagine first.

You have permission to drop your big heads on my shoulder with all their weight—I have two just for you—and lean in until your souls feel their rest. They will never be too heavy.

Imagine first.

DENNIS MAURICE

You have permission to use my advice (or not) as you need it and call on me as much as you please.

I can stretch myself far and wide, but I cannot imagine for you. You must find your keys and unlock everything you want in this life. The world ain't give it, and the world cannot take it away—it is yours.

You are not required to be anything other than who you are. He is enough. I do not want you to survive this life, I want you to lead it. That is a big job and what you carry may be too heavy for you, but it will never be too heavy for **US**. You are not heavy; you are my brothers.

I love you to the moon and back, infinity times, times ten…billion,

Denny

BLACK WASHED | *A Collection of Essays, Poems, Dreams, and Letters Addressed to Black Folk*

My brothers, Devin and Dylan—Photography credit: Darryl Cobb, Jr. (2017)

DENNIS MAURICE

The Back of the Spoon

A Reflection Addressed to Black Folk

BLACK WASHED | *A Collection of Essays, Poems, Dreams, and Letters Addressed to Black Folk*

The Back of the Spoon

"To be a negro in this country and to be relatively conscious is to be in a rage almost all the time."
-James Baldwin

I love this Baldwin quote and it outfits my temperament as a Black man of relative consciousness perfectly. I recognized how rage moved in my life well after meeting joy…
Joy and I go way back.

I was about five years old when I first recognized that love was more powerful than a home-cooked meal. Before that time, I conflated love with the passionate whisking of sweet potatoes, butter, eggs, cream, warm spices, and sugar for pie. Seeing my mother or grandmother's arms move and wrist flick ensuring there ain't *neary-a-lump* to be found. Washing the fibrous potato threads from the mixing blade safeguarding our family's good name with smooth pie poon was love to my young eyes.

I called myself helping my grandmother and aunt in our small 8by8 kitchen (more like taking up space and taste-testing everything). I had the distinct privilege of doing the least yet announcing that love was being served. And I would offer the most fraudulently fatigued "Dinner ready, y'all…" a five-year-old actor could muster. Then I would sway back and forth into the kitchen with a proud chin and hands full with the most anticipated dishes and pans. I was not mimicking their manner; I was echoing the response to the call of love cooked up in an 8by8 kitchen.

Everybody is grubbin'.

"Food must be good. Y'all quieter than the mice."

I have three spaces to live during dinner—under the table with my cousin, on the piano bench, or in the kitchen with the chefs. The day I first saw love I was in the kitchen. My mom made me a full plate with a little of everything. And I'm getting down, chyyy… going between my fork and my fingers as utensils.

Con. Sumed. by this plate, you hear me…

I took a moment to look up and noticed that none of the chefs were eating. "Mom-mom, Ro-Ro, why y'all not eating no chicken?" They chuckled and replied, "I been tasting along the way…ain't really hungry now. I'll get something after everybody else eat."

DENNIS MAURICE

I did not buy it—and I did not expect there to be any leftovers for them. So, I slowed up my eating pattern and scrutinized their actions; waiting for confirmation via the protest from their hungry bellies that they were all liars… fibbers… telling stories.

Instead, I recognized the deep joy as they talked with each other. I recognized how they took turns to see if everybody had enough or if anyone needed something else. I recognized how my grandmother had a small pot of stewed chicken simmering just in case somebody needed more. Their love was abundant. The details of their care were practiced and, in a way, scientific. And yet they were satisfied by the taste from the back of a spoon. In an odd marriage, the love they gave was also the love that fueled.

Today, I recognize that cooking a good meal ain't love.

The attention and intention we place into the meal; the care we are offering to someone else; the intimate occasion we willingly share to feed more than us is the mansion where love resides.

I knew love and joy well before I knew rage and hate.

And I met love and joy on the back of the spoon.

BLACK WASHED | *A Collection of Essays, Poems, Dreams, and Letters Addressed to Black Folk*

NOBODY SLEEP *Two*

> "People get used to anything.
> The less you think about your oppression the more your tolerance grows.
> After a while, people just think oppression is the normal state of things.
> But to become FREE, you have to be acutely aware of being a slave."
> **- Assata Shakur**

Our elder, Assata, frames this chapter so well. Our tolerance, while understandable, is irrational and unduly augmented. Our ability to compartmentalize, rationalize, and utilize this constructed reality birthed from the minds of soul-ill, irresponsible white men—so mentally sick that they demanded stolen people on peculated land refer to them as their first fathers—is a bizarre, grotesque vulgarity.

The truth is we are all conscious of the hostility of this condition.
We are awake.
We are alive in this skin.
As are they.
Ain't nobody sleep.

Welcome to Chapter two: Nobody Sleep—Foreword Author: Joy V. Harris.

DENNIS MAURICE

Two

Foreword Author

Joy V. Harris

Joy V. Harris, a Philadelphia native, creative, musician, and educator, earned three degrees in Special, Elementary, and Early Childhood Education from Lincoln University of Pennsylvania that led her to begin a career as an educator and servant leader.

After her time as a classroom teacher in Philadelphia and Chester, Pennsylvania, she began a new stage of her career working with communities of people that require mental health support. She has spent more than 15 years developing her unique approach to service and care that centers love, sound, and access to energy.

She is also a talented producer, musician, and singer and she plays the drums with passion and leads the worship experience at her church in Philadelphia. Moreover, Joy enjoys using her hands creatively through woodworking, writing poetry, and arranging melodies. In her free time, Joy loves to travel, which has included a three-month voyage throughout Europe and road trips across the country.

A Triptych:
She Understood.
We Know.
A Beat Black.
Joy V. Harris

She Understood

I never knew I needed to be cleansed
I found my joy in the prayers of my grandmother
in the spirit of church claps and foot stomps
family gatherings
the success of my peers
laughter and love making
meditation
fine wine and good sleep
But then
stormy and brewed
truth misconstrued
I woke up that morning
drowning in
her name Sandra
and it forced me to unplug
to debug
because I'm not wired to continuously download bullshit
she and me had been downloading the same input for the last 200+ years
since the middle passage
beaten and raped to work for free
breaking up our families
murdering our babies
stripping us of our dignity
exploited
ridiculed
stealing our cells while keeping us in cells
constantly dying so that others can live
we're always expected to give and to give and
to give
it's over kill
and overload
America's sin is this stain on the soul
Until it can acknowledge the truth of then and now

Leave me the FUCK alone.

DENNIS MAURICE

We Know

So, how do we cleanse?
I asked them two

                                                                Sabriya and Devyn

us 3 on the drive down 95 south
headed to bless our strengths

                                                                           Mother's Day

music blasted
thoughts loud in heavy
remembering and honoring those
roots colored purple

                                                       we still had a long way to go

Still thinking

                                         Ida Mae, was our great grandmother
                     ran a country stop sign and the police followed her
                                              until she confidently
                                          pulled into her yard
                          got out of her car and went into her house
                     instructing that boy, "you best get out my yard"
                                        She didn't get a ticket

She was our hidden figure and so were they
running stop signs

                                                                       She told them to go

now doctors
bobbing their heads and reciting lyrics to trap music
the beat was hard too

I smiled
Looking past the moon and thinking to myself
Black women must be from that planet behind the sun and closest to GOD

BLACK WASHED | *A Collection of Essays, Poems, Dreams, and Letters Addressed to Black Folk*

A Beat Black

this beat be original
no sampling here
although they try
her measure is never caught
She was given a rhythm that only She can understand and dance to
                                                                                                                                                           call it a signature

patterns patented in HIS image
her form was created
from there She birth forth life
rippling syncopated accents in the down beats
forced to ghost
and be the decrescendo
while continuously being beat on
She beat on
knowing that her sound is the most important part of the track

catch that beat Black?
they banned that
brought that back
cross her back
still no slack
catch that beat Black

DENNIS MAURICE

She swing that beat

her beat beautifully Black
loud proud
intentional
the effects of her symbol
never ceasing nor silent
after all
She is a healer of self
a healer of people
magical in strength
setting her own tempo
a right
gifted to her in the vibrations of those who drummed before her
She is sacred
Her truth cannot be stopped or quieted
this beat be original

BLACK WASHED | *A Collection of Essays, Poems, Dreams, and Letters Addressed to Black Folk*

Something to Cry About

A Dream for Black Kids

Something to Cry About

We don't need no more alters to prey on Black youth.
We don't need no more sitters standing on their backs for 8 hours cancelling their right to breathe.
We don't need no more pigeonholes that place their energy in miniature cages labeled anxiety.
We lay Black kids prostrate on barbed roads to protect the tractors that will dig their graves.

If you don't fix your Gahtdam face…
Have folk in here thinking I'm hurting you.
Ya ass don't know hurt…yet.
But trust and believe I can give ya ass something to cry about…

We force Black kids to use their developing Black genius for survival in this American horror story.
We urge them to learn how to apply to schools before applying themselves.
We encourage them to go into financially abusive institutions that can't afford them.
We tell them that their dreams can fly, but their gear can't be.
We indoctrinate toddlers into a capitalistic world and then tell them…
'don't touch nothing. don't look at nothing.'
We continue to give them something to cry about.
Black kids got to be out of tears.

I dream that we love us so much that we can't bear to see our children looking like anyone else…
I dream that Black kids think humbleness is a pejorative and their magic is restorative.
I dream that Black kids learn history from me and not in Classroom 203.
I dream that Black kids know more than lack and always have McDonald's money, and…
I also dream that Black kids eat from a free lunch that we cooked
…in our own pot.

But trust and believe I can give ya ass something to cry about…
Ya ass don't know hurt…yet.
Have folk in here thinking I'm hurting you.
If you don't fix your Gahtdam face…

BLACK WASHED | *A Collection of Essays, Poems, Dreams, and Letters Addressed to Black Folk*

Black kids are grieving and we're editing the messages their tears are writing on our tombstone.
Stout Black kids are fighting Debo to keep the chains their grandparents gave them.
Stout Black kids are winning battles their parents didn't teach them how to fight.
Stout Black kids are watching as we sing songs about stealing their bodies and celebrate the thieves.
And when they wail a battle cry for their victory we respond 'I can give you something cry about…'
As if Black kids got any more tears to give at this point.

My dream for Black kids is also a decree:
I pray with all the trials you face; you won't find one in me.
I pray that older folk guard your brilliance and bodies like we do our coldest, darkest testimony.
We've given you a lot to cry about and I want us to write a new story.

Black child my dream is that we proudly write your name down…not off
Black child my dream is that we offer you sanctuaries and carnivals
Black child my dream is that we crown you…not drown you
Black child my dream is that you don't have survivors' remorse at age 15…
I dream…
That we don't stand on your backs and criticize your posture
That we love you when you sag and lift you when you slack
That we honor the beauty of being young, gifted, and Black.

It is time to give you directions without showing you our backs.

DENNIS MAURICE

G.R.I.T.S.

A Pot of Thought Gumbo Addressed to Black Folk

(written in 2015)

G.R.I.T.S.

Nobody makes grits like me. They are creamy, buttery, luxury in a steaming hot pot with a flavor unlike any other you will taste. It starts with roasting a chicken—yes, I need to roast a whole damn bird to make grits.

"Roast one cut-up whole (four pound) chicken at 400 degrees for one-hour and 20 minutes (seasoned with a blend salt, pepper, smoked paprika, honey, chopped garlic, juice from half a lemon, rosemary, garlic & onion powders, and mix that with a stick of softened butter & one tablespoon of olive oil. Rub that bird down; on and under the skin.)

Take the chicken out and reserve the sumptuous stock that developed in the pan. Sometimes I blend it just to make sure it doesn't have any big pieces of garlic or herbs in it. You can put the chicken back in for 15 minutes, uncovered to brown if you would like to eat on it later.

Now you are going to pour the stock into a big pot (usually yields at least 2 cups) and add a cup of water and bring that to a boil at medium-high heat. At that point you want to whisk in 1 cup of heavy cream or half & half.

Now whisk in 1 ½ cup of 5-minute grits (whisking is important, so your grits don't clump) and you whisk until the fast-popping boil turns into a gentle rage.

Turn your heat down to medium-low and continue whisking every 4-5 minutes until you start to see a creamy consistency. At that point turn it down low and cover your grits and cook them for about 30 minutes (check them to make sure they're not sticking). And voila you will have an amazingly rich pot of grits, baby."

You can learn a lot from cooking grits. My favorite part of cooking them is the gentle rage while it is boiling. I love it because you see it bubble, but you have no idea that the grits are blossoming and they are taking in the melody of flavors, engaging with every new note. In just a little while that humble pot will turn into the richest part of your meal. And when you taste it, it is like a spoonful of salvation, because this lowly dish done turned itself into a meal fit for folk ready to heal.

This world is like my grits—without as much good taste. It is a bubbling mass of ideas, identities, and beliefs that are always tangled in a *gentle rage with an intense taste of salvation* (g.r.i.t.s.). Everything is coming together amid a violent and necessary bubbling that must happen to get to the bountiful harmony birthed from our meager grains.

Rage is uncomfortable. Rage is terrifying. Rage must be felt.

Today, we are reckoning with years of shrouded rage that has been paraded as good will and now, unresolved, the rage becomes less and less gentle. Anything that is left in the pot too long will burn. Everything will burn the longer we let it sit and fester without any intention of atonement. If you have ever burned something in a pot, it is almost impossible to get that scent out of it. You will always have at least a hint of the burning linger. And the stains will never be gone.

At the end of the day, we just a pot of grits, but we have been cooking too long.

And anything you leave on the fire too long will burn. Everything will burn.

***

Author's Note: I wrote G.R.I.T.S. in 2015 soon after the birth of the Black Lives Matter movement. I was going to leave this out, but in the context of 2020 and beyond this has proven itself accurate and monotonous in ways that are unfortunately disturbing and reliable. The concept of America does not need another think piece to validate it. However, I added this reflection or "Pot of Thought Gumbo" to this version of *Black Washed*, because it is stunning how much repetition we live in. Sometimes I feel like we are having the same fights with the same devils and their same old tricks. It may be time to let this pot burn.

BLACK & EMPTY
Three

My emptiness is a sanctuary.

Empty things have room to hold. I have been taught to dishonor my emptiness. I have treated my empty parts like a thief of progress, pleasure, and atonement. That is a lie. It was when I felt Godless that I made room for deeper connections with what lives in me. It was when I lost loved ones that I found room to shadow their legacy. It was when I was penniless that I learned how luxurious gratitude feels. It was when I emptied all the rooms that I could furnish the home.

My emptiness is a sanctuary.

Welcome to Chapter three: Black & Empty—Foreword Author: Ivory Allison.

DENNIS MAURICE

Three

Foreword Author

Ivory Allison

Ivory is a Black woman who owes her life to the contributions Black women sowed into her—namely her mother, aunt, and grandmother. She is a native Philadelphian who was raised by her single mother in West and South Philadelphia. She graduated from West Catholic High School and Saint Joseph's University with a B.S. in Sociology. Although her commitment to Philadelphia is well documented, Ivory has expanded her horizons by studying abroad in Sydney/Melbourne, Australia.

In 2004, her mother passed away and she took on the responsibility at 24 on raising her 12-year-old sister. Without the love of her aunt and grandmother and the core values that her mother instilled in her, she didn't know how she'd make it, but she not only survived, her and her sister thrived. Ivory Allison is an accomplished executive in the nonprofit industry with outstanding credentials and a proven record of results. In 2006, after more than five years of dedicated service from everything from an event coordinator to the Director of Events, Ivory was appointed as Vice-President of Programming and Production for the nation's premiere Independence Day celebration, Sunoco Welcome America! She is widely known to many as the 'go-to-woman' for her strong expertise in event planning/production. In 2007 she represented the City of Philadelphia at the 49th Annual Grammy Awards and in Athens, Greece for the International Festival & Events Association.

She was appointed the first African American Executive Director of the American Liver Foundation, Mid-Atlantic Division in November 2011 after joining the organization in 2010 and currently is the first and only African American Executive at the American Liver Foundation national level. She was listed as one of the 10 people under 40 to watch in 2007 by the Philadelphia Tribune Newspaper, listed as one of the African American leaders in the City of Philadelphia from 2016-2020 and one of the Women of Distinction for the Philadelphia Business Journal. Ivory has cultivated an amazing career and the best part is it is just beginning.

Wash Us

Ivory Allison

BLACK WASHED | *A Collection of Essays, Poems, Dreams, and Letters Addressed to Black Folk*

Black Woman.
Black Woman is Me.
Black Woman is Life.
Since the beginning of time Black Women have washed humanity. Washed Black children, washed Black men, washed white children, washed white women, and their white men.
We've washed with our love, compassion, kindness, sorrow, pain, grief, joy, and power. **WASH US.**

My mother, aunt, and grandmother washed me into the woman I am today, and their spirits continue to wash me. It was not a daily washing, but when they washed me, I always felt like new. A new person that could be anyone and do anything. **WASH US.**

If not for the washing through their love, laughter, knowledge, heartache, sadness, and sometimes agony, I could not walk out my door every day ready to face the world. They washed me up and then wrapped me in confidence, beauty, strength, and the courage to be a conqueror. **WASH US.**

Wash us with your respect.
Wash us by not fearing us.
Wash us with support.
Wash us with your positive energy.
Wash us with your kindness.
Wash us with your smile.
Wash us without condemning us.

It's proven that whether you wash Black Women or not our magic will never be diminished, and we will continue to wash the world with love. Black women are this world's truest expression of love. Respect our integrity and glory and when you are blessed to have Black Women pour our love onto you, recognize that there is **NOTHING** on this earth as powerful and magical as that nourishment.
Her nourishment enhances life.

WASH US.

DENNIS MAURICE

Body Heat

A Poem Addressed to Black

Body Heat

Some like it hot.

I like it warm.

I like to feel the heat, but not too much, just right. You know?

That is why my head finds creative positions on your lap when we are together.

Because my heart grows cold when we secretly comment under 97-week-old Instagram posts.

Or argue over the phone about something pointless that I made up because I have not yet mastered how to be human enough to tell you that I really need your body and your heat next to me.

My thumbs hurt from typing and re-typing long text messages to you…

Messages that eventually get deleted and replaced with 'Whatever…'

But what I really wanted to say was…

I love you.

And it feels real now.

And I want to have pretty Black babies with you…
Black babies with skin that require copious amounts of moisturizers, shea butter, and coconut oil
Black babies that gnaw on half eaten chicken bones instead of teething rings…

And I want to say that you make me feel good inside.

And I have grown dependent on your heat to get through the day.

I don't just want you.

I need you…

My spirit craves your warmth.

Every part of me is aroused when you're near…

Not because you're the sexiest… but because every time I am near you and feel your body's heat, I want to fall deep into you and drink you like cocoa.

I am in love with your cocoa.

But instead, I settle for… 'Whatever…'

Because allowing you to know that your body heat is necessary may make you feel yourself

And if you feel yourself too much you might get greedy and start giving your heat away…

And then I will have to fight them for all the warm spaces that I want close.

So instead, I act like it's just… 'Whatever…'

But that 'Whatever…' does not give me you.

In fact, it separates us and kills our magic.

You don't even know that I need your magic.

You don't even know that I see your magic.

You don't even know that we are magic.

Because I refuse to request your body heat

Because I refuse to look thirsty

When the truth is, I feel uncomfortable and icy without your warmth.

But why can't I tell you that your electricity moves me?

That your warmth feels like the prayers I prayed…

Your heat is anointing me.

All I can muster is "Whatever?!"

I gotta let you know your heat is spiritual.
I gotta let you know your heat is beautiful.
I gotta let you know your heat is magical.
I gotta let you know your heat is…

Whatever.

BLACK WASHED | *A Collection of Essays, Poems, Dreams, and Letters Addressed to Black Folk*

All Fourths Matter

An Essay Addressed to Black Folk

All Fourths Matter

I am writing this on July 4, and I am thinking deeply about America and Freedom and the long history of American fourths.

I am meditating on **January 4th, 1923** when gangs of racist white men gathered around the home of Sarah Carrier and shot her in the head while the young Black children in her family visiting for Christmas watched. This happened during the seven days of white terror known as the Rosewood Massacres occurred, which left this tight knit Black community devastated, burned down, and destroyed. Their cabins and homes were set on fire and the white mob killed 20 Black people and injured many more. These Black folk in Rosewood did nothing more than pull themselves up by their bootstraps (as we are often told to do) and built a thriving Black community for themselves. Despite their hard work and ascension to freedom and liberation their lives were destroyed by an American idea of Freedom, centered in white supremacist terror. This is the America I live in.

I am meditating on **February 4, 2014** when 16 missing children and 50 women were rescued after being forced into a Super Bowl sex & human-trafficking ring that still exists today. The Super Bowl sex trafficking ring was so big that there was a suspected 10,000 women and children being illegally trafficked to and from Super Bowl locations, internationally. Today large major events in the US are the biggest opportunities for slavery, trafficking, rape, and molestation in the country. While police are militarized to gas and terrorize peaceful protestors, they've yet to be deployed to capture sex offenders in this American Slave Trade complex. This is the America I live in.

I am meditating on **March 4, 1789**, when the first U.S. Congress met, establishing the US Constitution and the first 10 Bill of Rights (proposed officially on September 25, 1789) were set. I must remember that on this fourth rights like the Freedom of Religion, Freedom of Speech, Freedom of Assembly, the Right to Petition the Government, were not extended to Black folk and ostracized Indigenous communities. Today, 231 years and four months later we still align ourselves with the mentalities of men that enslaved, persecuted, and killed people you say were their fellow Americans. Today, America and its accomplices still ask why Black & Indigenous folk and POC see its forefathers on monuments as anti-American hate symbols. Today, we still struggle to question the vile, inhumane condition America's fathers left as inheritance. This is the America I live in.

I am meditating on **April 4, 1968** when civil rights icon and nonviolent movement leader, Rev. Dr. Martin Luther King, Jr., was assassinated by racist, white terrorist, James Earl Ray. I am meditating on how America's racism has made a practice of assassinating Black bodies and voices. I meditate on the fact that I live in a country that has centered the public murder of Black bodies at the hands of white 'supremacy' for centuries. I meditate on the fact that social justice and new era movement leaders have been thrusted into elderhood in their 30s and 40s, because so many prior have been killed while fighting for Black freedom or due to being disinvested from the humanity that America reserves for its chosen.

I am meditating on **May 4, 1961** when Freedom Riders rode in a silent protest through confederate states against their refusal to desegregate public buses. I am reminded of how Birmingham's Police Commissioner, Bull Connor, and vocal Ku Klux Klan supporter & Police Sergeant, Tom Cook, ordered a mob of deranged white men to throw firebombs into their bus and then blocked the door to murder them in that burning vehicle. It would have worked if not for an explosion that forced the deranged white mob to retreat.

I am meditating on **June 4, 1919** when the 19th Amendment was approved by the senate allowing white women the full right to vote. It is not lost on me that 50 years later Black folk would still be fighting for the right to vote without suppression. It is not lost on me that 100 years after suffrage, this American freedom is still not fully afforded to Black folk. This country still grapples with ensuring anti-racist systems that protect us all from suppression like we have seen in Georgia, Florida, Kentucky, and other states recently.

I am meditating on **August 4, 1964** when young Civil Rights Workers, Michael Schwerner, Andrew Goodman (both white men), and James Earl Chaney (a Black man), were found buried after being murdered by gun shot a month prior at the hands of the White Knights of the Ku Klux Klan members in Philadelphia, Mississippi. This is widely known as the Freedom Summer Murders or the Mississippi Burning Murders. The men were visiting the town to speak at a Black Church that had just been burned down. Upset with the men in their town, 18 convicted and alleged white men and women (7 received minor sentences), affiliated with the White Knights of the KKK burned their vehicle, shot the men, and buried them. One man, Edgar Ray Killen, was convicted of manslaughter 41 years later and died in jail in 2018 at the age of 92. The last time Chaney (21), Goodman (20), and Schwerner (24) were seen alive was during a traffic stop by police in Mississippi.

I am meditating on **September 4, 1957** when Governor Orval Faubus directed the Arkansas National Guard to block the entry of the Black students who would integrate one of Little Rock's most prominent high schools. The Black students, known as the Little Rock Nine, were signed up to integrate the previously all-white Little Rock Central High School by the NAACP. Governor Faubus in a televised address to the citizens of Arkansas said, "Blood will run in the streets if Negro pupils should attempt to enter Central High School." On September 25, 1957, the Little Rock Nine had to attend Central High School under the protection of the 101st Airborne Division and Federal Troops deployed by President Eisenhower to protect them from the community of violent, deranged white adults and children. I meditate as today we see this hatred for Black children in schools mutated into an environment that over-polices, disinvests Black families and poor communities from resources, and still refuses to integrate a stable educational funding pipeline for schools serving Black children.

I am meditating on **October 4, 1951** when Henrietta Lacks (born Loretta Pleasant) died from cervical cancer after going to Johns Hopkins Hospital in Baltimore for help. Johns Hopkins' Dr. George Otto Gey used Lacks' cells and named them **HeLa** (**He**nrietta **La**cks) **cells** without her or her family's permission & while she was fighting cancer. These cells were used to find the vaccine for Polio and aiding in research for cancer, diabetes, and other diseases. Her stolen cells were distributed and, in

some cases sold for medical research and yet with all this rich value she still died in the care of the medical professionals that would later steal what was left of her. I am reminded how the Black body, especially the bodies of Black women, are used without question or permission. Henrietta Lacks died at the age of 31 and was buried in an unmarked grave after staying in the hospital for two months.

I am meditating on **November 4, 1980** when Ronald Reagan was elected as president and immediately started crippling poor and non-white communities through Reaganomics and the War on Drugs. What we know today, especially after hearing recordings from Lee Atwater that detail the maniacal, deceptive, racist intentions of these conservative political movements under Nixon, Reagan, Bush, and later by Democrat President Bill Clinton is that it was designed to kill and destroy Black people. I am meditating on how much evil he and other white men in power have orchestrated in communities like my hometown of Philadelphia, PA, that has still not reconciled or repaired today.

I am meditating on **December 4, 1969** when Fred Hampton and Mark Clark, leaders of Black Panther Party were assassinated by the Chicago Police Department. Mark Clark was shot at point blank range in the head as he worked security detail for their home. After being drugged with Barbiturates, Fred Hampton (unarmed) was shot by the officers somewhere between 90–99 times, in a clear assassination, while he laid on the bed with his fiancée, Deborah Johnson, who was nine-months pregnant. It is not lost on me that we continue to see this same type of attack on Black liberation throughout history—Martin Luther King, Jr. (assassinated the year prior), Medgar Evers (assassinated in 1963), and the MOVE Bombing in Philadelphia, which assassinated adults and children in 1985. Black liberation is so feared in this country that anyone advocating for it, historically, has been killed—many times by the police.

BLACK WASHED | *A Collection of Essays, Poems, Dreams, and Letters Addressed to Black Folk*

So today, **July 4th, 2020**, as this country swaddles its nasty, bigot womb in red, white, and blue and praises American freedom, I meditate on how none of it applies to me. Daily and annually, this country chooses, to thank a mix of slave owners, racists, and murderers and name them our fathers. Daily and annually picking away at attempts to heal like a scab, until blood and skin switch position. A nation so dedicated to revisionism that it has national holidays to celebrate self-erected, yet impotent, and embezzled freedom to walk on robbed land *and backs*, while abusing the inventions and bodies of stolen people is at the very least corrupt.

This is Americana.
This is America.
This is sickness.
There are no vertebrae.
Spineless.

I am reminding myself that #AllFourthsMatter and I choose to employ today as a point of reflection on the legacy of America as a country founded on xenophobia, racism, misogyny, patriarchy, anti-Blackness, peculation, oppression, and slavery.

There is no feast for me at your picnic table of unseasoned forgeries committed by 'forefathers' who made sure their children ate and left the rest of us with the bill. I am making the choice to redecorate July 4th and remind myself that it is just another day in this vile, barbaric, racist America.

And this is where I live. I live in this America. And, for me, these fourths are nothing to celebrate.

DENNIS MAURICE

Decolonizing Romance

A Reflection Addressed to Black Folk

Decolonizing Romance

She said "Be careful, I love you…" before I walked out the door.

She rarely said it, but I always felt it. She was love.

My mind heard her before my feet, so I kept walking while my mind went on a romantic voyage. I thought about the abundance of her love, but my feet kept walking away from her magic and medicine, out of her warm home, across her loving threshold, and into cold winds and colder hands.

Romance.

I was a teen when I first felt those cold winds and colder hands caress my chubby boy chest. The same titties I was shamed for and used my arms and double layered shirts to cover up were now impressive monuments worthy of colder hands made warm by my appreciation. My head could not hear anything after those colder hands touched me. Romance.

They spoke a different language and I proudly chose to hear his sweet, warm touch instead.

He was romance.

Before too long I offered more than my chubby boy chest to those colder hands and soon it seemed like every part of my body had new ears and it all heard the same proudly chosen, sweet, warm embrace. Before too long cold winds and colder hands felt like a new home, being outside felt better than being in and I was ready to give away my old ears to hear a new thing. Romance.

One day I was outside far from her home with only cold winds and his colder hands to keep me company. I had no money and new ears that only seemed to work when his colder hands were near.

This was romance.

We began to walk, not sure where we were going. We stopped along the way to find warm spaces in each other and before I knew it, we were approaching her home. I could smell her magic and medicine from the corner of the block. And although I had these new ears all over my body, my feet heard a familiar love calling me, a real love I had traded in for romantic colder hands with a proudly chosen, sweet, warm embrace. My feet heard what the rest of me could not.

Romance.

I finished my voyage walking away from his colder hands, out of those cold winds, across her loving threshold, and back into her warm home.

Now, I am in my warm, loving bed wishing for colder hands again.

BLACK WASHED | *A Collection of Essays, Poems, Dreams, and Letters Addressed to Black Folk*

BETWEEN HANDS & CLAY

Four

> "won't you celebrate with me
> what i have shaped into
> a kind of life? i had no model.
> born in Babylon
> both nonwhite and woman
> what did i see to be except myself?
> i made it up
> here on this bridge between starshine and clay,
> my one hand holding tight my other hand;
> come celebrate with me that everyday
> something has tried to kill me
> and has failed."
>
> -Lucille Clifton (won't you celebrate with me from *Book of Light* ©1993)

Welcome to Chapter four: Between Hands & Clay—Foreword Author: Dreena Whitfield-Brown.

DENNIS MAURICE

BLACK WASHED | *A Collection of Essays, Poems, Dreams, and Letters Addressed to Black Folk*

Four

Foreword Author

Dreena Whitfield-Brown

Dreena Whitfield-Brown is the founder and CEO of the New Jersey-based public relations and strategic communications firm, WhitPR. Born in Newark and raised in Westfield, this New Jersey native is a new-ish mommy, navigating the demands of a booming Black business. A savvy Jersey Girl, Dreena earned her Bachelor of Science degree in Mass Communications from Lincoln University of Pennsylvania.

A daughter of a single parent home, Dreena learned independence at an early age and attributes her success to her mother. "My mother worked three jobs consecutively at one point to care for my brother and me," she says. "It's from her that I developed my work ethic. She is the hardest working woman I know, and I wouldn't be who I am without her. She always taught us to not give up, have faith, and pray through the good and bad times. I started WhitPR in my living room in 2009; with no clients, no media contacts, and no professional mentors—but my mother's wisdom has always lifted me up."

Today, Dreena juggles her burgeoning Black-owned business with a robust portfolio of domestic clients with international reach along with her young son and husband. In all Dreena's work she centers the business and elevation of Black voices, Black women, and movements, deliberately.

You can hear more about Dreena's perspectives on her podcast, <u>How I Got Here with Dreena Whitfield</u>, available on all streaming platforms.

DENNIS MAURICE

This is Magic
Dreena Whitfield-Brown

BLACK WASHED | *A Collection of Essays, Poems, Dreams, and Letters Addressed to Black Folk*

I built a business on the importance of elevating and amplifying the stories of Black women. A common, yet unfortunate, thread among these women—each a successful powerhouse in her own right—is they must continue to prove ownership of their expertise, regardless of their success. Whether it is from men, other women, or their respective industries, they have all had experiences where their work has been diminished, co-opted, and overlooked. As a successful Black woman that works closely with successful Black women, I recognize what we do to navigate these inequitable systems as we build our careers and lives. I have noticed that there is often a need and hunger to overcompensate, overwork, and go to great, sometimes unreasonable lengths, to prove our worth. Regardless of what the world may misinterpret or not value about us, I am clear that Black women are pure magic—I know that's cliché, but we know it is the truth. And what makes us extraordinary is our **strength, integrity, and perseverance** (I call that the Black Girl's S.I.P.).

It was not until I became a grown woman with a career and full life that I realized the strong Black womanhood I inherited. I have always known something was uniquely precious about me and the women that lifted my Black girl magic, but it was truly an aha moment (cue an Oprah scream) when I entered the workforce and had to access my gifts. The world understands the brilliance of Black women and the need for us to be at the table but does not often value who is sitting in that seat.

I remember early in my career, while working in a highly visible role, a white counterpart of mine inferred that I was in my position because of connections. I worked hard prior to that role with large corporations, freelancing, and grinding and I had the experience to be there. I was hurt, infuriated, and offended and I replied to him, *"Please don't think your resume trumps mine, because it doesn't. I've worked just as hard as you to be here."* It was in this moment that I realized that regardless of my hard work and strength, to him, I was a tokened Black girl available for appearances and not content. At that moment, my fight rose, and I knew I had to aggressively create a path and presence that made me irreplaceable. Moving forward he unfairly monitored my every step, encroached on every accomplishment I secured, and simply refused to value or trust me. Regardless I pushed myself to be better than the environment, strong-willed, and overly prepared—whether sick or tired, I was going to show up and shine bright. But why did I have to show up and shine for someone who had no intention on seeing my light?

This is just one example of an experience that Black women go through all the time. It was a difficult experience, but I was raised right. I did what I saw my mother, a strong Black woman, do my entire life—I figured it out. I figured out a way to make sense of that experience and how to show up dazzling with undeniable Black girl sparkle (and my S.I.P.). And despite the dim experience I was having I accessed my magic just as my mother taught me.

DENNIS MAURICE

If I look back to my childhood, I honestly do not know how my mother did it. She moved mountains to ensure I had my needs and wants. And essentially, like my mother, that is what makes Black women magical, because we always get it done without permission, often without guidance, or an idea of where/when/how to start. There are no tears (publicly), just courage & hustle. Throughout my life, personally and professionally, I have called on the magic my mother stored inside of me to make it through and ease the doubts about whether my gifts were mystical or mythical.

My magic stems from my mother. I was raised by a woman who was unapologetic in her quest to provide for her children in the upper middle-class town of Westfield, New Jersey—where seventeen-year-old affluent children are gifted BMW's and luxury vacations for their birthdays. My mother was one of the first African American meter maids for the town and worked two to three jobs at times so that my brother and I could have access to quality education and resources. And despite the diverted paths of life, she ultimately became the first African American town clerk for the building department (responsible for millions of dollars in development funding).

Her endurance and ability to break down barriers are the roots that have helped me grow into the woman I am today. In her living I gained an inheritance that keeps me both grounded and elevated as a strong, magical Black woman. Regarding *Black Washed* and the question of how the world can wash Black women I offer this statement: Black women do not need to be "washed," we need to be trusted, we need to be acknowledged, and we need to be valued.

When you meet magic, you better welcome being in awe of her. Treat Black women like the magical vessels we are and nothing less. Now let's S.I.P., Black Girls.

BLACK WASHED | *A Collection of Essays, Poems, Dreams, and Letters Addressed to Black Folk*

For These Porcelain Harbors

Venting with Black Folk trying their best to not lose themselves in white spaces.

DENNIS MAURICE

For These Porcelain Harbors

For more than 15 years I worked as a nonprofit fundraiser. I have been invited into the homes of more than a few affluent families (mostly white people and/or folk who revel in capitalism). One of the things I have noticed is that many of them have a similar collection of porcelain, fine, or bone china tea sets with delicately portrayed white men and women standing in front of harbored ships painted on them.

It was not uncommon for us to have little in common.

To relieve the awkwardness, I would remark or celebrate what I saw in their homes as a point of engaging with them. I noticed a reoccurring trend were donors having a version of this signature porcelain harbor tea set in their homes. I would ask them what historic event was being portrayed on the porcelain surfaces. Without fail they would proudly tell me a story of heroic, majestic theft, conquering, or disruption at a harbor being captured on these delicate surfaces. The images, annoyingly unassuming, generally depicted stately, calm, antiquated white people living beautiful lives with ships moored to harbors.

I grew frustrated that I chose a profession where people's heritage and wealth accumulation allowed them to celebrate stolen harbors and destroyed land on porcelain saucers over tea. I would always excuse myself to the bathroom, so I can properly mind my manners. I would offer myself a short period to vent about engaging with white-centered sensibilities. One day after seeing a new set of porcelain harbors, I spent minutes venting via whispers into my voice recorder in a washroom:

BLACK WASHED | *A Collection of Essays, Poems, Dreams, and Letters Addressed to Black Folk*

Lord, help me find the peace of mind to no longer search for these porcelain harbors.

Ads for historical horrors proudly locked in china safes like impotent erections that can no longer feel pleasure are broadcasted while I tout unmet Black needs in exchange for checks.

This feels inadequate at best and I am lost in a gutter of do-gooders who honor a lineage of feckless, Western thieves and various manner of deplorables,
while we discuss how their gift will inspire a community more honorable… and more just.

At this point, I guess I am one with whiteness, it finds comfort in me, especially;
My lips part in ways that keep it comfortable,
and my phrasing shows I am an unassuming expert in the Anglo-polyglot.

I am lost in a sea of porcelain harbors and ships that trafficked my ancestors and stole their gifts.

I am anchored to these depictions of terrorized shores like a ball and chain and well fastened moors.

Lord, help me find the peace of mind to no longer search for these porcelain harbors.

Update: I am no longer searching for these porcelain harbors.

DENNIS MAURICE

Resting My Eyes

A Concept Addressed to Black Folk who confuse locked emotions with safe spaces.

Resting My Eyes

There are four types of tears, but generally only three are acknowledged (possibly because I thought of the fourth category in a dark room fighting five years of stored spiritual ache. Who knows?!):

> **Emotional Tears:** Tears made when one is overcome with emotion.
> **Reflex Tears:** Tears made when the body needs to respond (example: an eyelash in your eye).
> **Basal Tears:** Tears made to protect the eye from drying out.

I spent the better part of the day crying. These are emotional tears. I cried so much that my emotional tears developed into reflex tears caused by constant eye rubbing that summoned a flood of protective tears. It continues. I continue with irritated, enflamed, basal tear-filled eyes.

Frustrated by my irritated eyes I become more emotional and return to the cycle of crying these three tears. The only way I know to stop this is sleep. I do not cry while I am sleeping and if I do, I am not aware, because I am… sleeping. I do not feel the tears or the roots that birthed them.

I cry myself to sleep as day transitions to night and wake up in a dark room. Disoriented. Unaware of whether I slept for 2 hours on a Sunday or if I slept straight into Monday night. Without a clear thought in my head, I begin to cry again. I am confused.

How can I wake up crying the tears I left behind? It hit me. There must be a fourth classification of tears—Stored Tears. The tears I have been holding in are fighting me for their freedom. And they win. No amount of sleep will stop this from reminding me of the *me* too humane to resolve.

I have not cried these three tears in five years, so stored tears broke free, releasing their chains in a slammer I created. No bond. Alone, yet vulnerable and ashamed of the years of captivity I condoned in this body, I went back to sleep. I was escaping the mess that was unpacking me, without *me*.

I wake up to a phone call from my mom. "Hey You! You sleep?"

"No, I'm just resting my eyes…"

"Well, it's time to get up."

EVERYTHING *Five* WILL BURN

> "No matter whether you fry or boil it…
> If you leave it in the pot too long…
> Everything will burn."
> **- Dennis Maurice**

Welcome to Chapter five: Everything Will Burn—Foreword Author: Gloria McNeil.

BLACK WASHED | *A Collection of Essays, Poems, Dreams, and Letters Addressed to Black Folk*

Five

Foreword Author

Gloria McNeil

Gloria McNeil is a native West Philadelphian. She is the proud mother and grandmother of three beautiful children and two grandchildren. Gloria has a passion for seeking the mysteries and revelation of The Lord Jesus Christ and utilizing the appropriate application of the Word of God.

My Personal Truth

Gloria McNeil

My Black teachers, who were once sweet and docile, became militant. We were drilled in Black history studies because we were told that we will always have to remember who we were and where we came from because one day "the world" was going to make us forget. We were inundated with examples of Black power and Black excellence. This was the premise that formulated my young mind's-perception of Black America.

During this time, our heroes were Martin Luther King, Ralph Bunche, George Washington Carver, Malcolm X, Thurgood Marshall, and Booker T. Washington.

During this time, we saw our Black preachers in the pulpits as people deserving of reverential respect.

During this time, the neighbors on our block were more like extended family members and when we had block parties, they were better than family reunions.

It was like our parents, grandparents, and ancestors who fought, bled, marched, and died, did not want us to see, touch, or taste the inequalities that they faced, so we partied our way through middle and high school totally unaware of what "the world" had in store for us.

It was not uncommon to see a father in the homes of our friends, even though it was starting to become sparse. The welfare system made it impossible for the Black family structure to survive with a Black man in the home and collect public assistance. So, if a family needed any financial assistance, which was the case for most Blacks in our neighborhood, the man had to be absent or removed from the home. So, when the Black man left the Black home, "the world" created a substitute for him.

They tried to give us Super Fly, the Mack, Shaft, and Dolemite. As this imagery hit our neighborhood movie theatres and were being imitated by some of the Baby Booming, displaced men; it did not escape the eyes of my immediate peers. We were able to see the buffoonery of it.

We also saw how ridiculous gang violence was. It did not make sense to us to murder someone because they didn't live in our neighborhood and stood at the corner of our block. We saw the importance of the Black Power Movement and decided that education was our key to success and getting out of the ghetto. We did not really want to stay and clean it up, we wanted to leave it because it represented everything, we presently did not like about ourselves and our environments; and we darn sure did not want to bring its stench into our future. So those who were able to get away, sprinted out of the ghetto. Those who stayed, partied, and boy did we party. We were now able to party without the restraints of the former generations. We did not have to worry about certain bad drugs. That is not to say that they weren't around and every now and then you would hear about someone being slipped a 'mickey,' but for the most part, we were relatively safe. We had Planned Parenthood, and if we made a 'mistake,' it could be taken care of. This is just the calm before the storm of what the world had in store for us.

BLACK WASHED | *A Collection of Essays, Poems, Dreams, and Letters Addressed to Black Folk*

We saw college as a real option due to the affirmative action programs, and we were qualified to not only attend, but to excel, because our militant elementary school teachers gave us an excellent academic foundation. Good Times, the television show, was entertainment, not prophetic. We were too old to accept any relevance to J.J. Walker. We saw through the veil that was being created for us through television. We did not want to marry the "prince" of the project complex. When James Evans lost his job repeatedly and finally died, we saw the symbolism attached to it. When they showed us images that implied we would never be able to have any strides in life and would have to hide all our new belongings when the evil caseworkers came into our homes, it did not move us. We just made plans to buy our parents new homes, cars, and possessions. What we did not prepare for was the storm that hit us—HIV/AIDS and crack cocaine.

I got married and left Philadelphia in the summer of 1983. Before I left, my friends were still smoking weed and partying. I started having babies, and I no longer had a desire to hang in the circles of my former friends. I was preparing a life for me and my family, so my focus was not on my surroundings. I remembered hearing that the mental institutions were being emptied out, and that the State did not place those residents in places that would assist them. I heard that those former residents were being kicked out onto the streets. At that time, I just looked at it as rumors. It never occurred to me that our neighbors were being desensitized to human suffering so that we would not be sympathetic to the plight of our fellow human beings.

When I left Philadelphia and moved to Germany, I did not know that I was also escaping the crack epidemic. Within the five years that I was away, I also lived in Oklahoma. I left Oklahoma right before crack hit Dell City. By the grace of God, I escaped the crack trap twice.

I returned to Philadelphia in the fall of 1988. Within that five-year span, crack destroyed my beloved community. My favorite childhood friend, who was gay, was addicted to crack, but also had contracted HIV & AIDS. I lost him in 1995. There were no longer any parties. There were only crack houses in the abandoned houses that were pulverized by the 'pipers' who emptied them out for a quick high. The elderly was no longer revered, burglary was rampant, and I was no longer in a place that I could call my home—I was in a warzone.

When people in mental health facilities were kicked out of those institutions, they lived on sidewalks and slowly became wallpaper. I can recall an incident when I saw one of my childhood buddies walking up the street toward my house. He had a supermarket shopping cart with him carrying all his belongings. He stopped to chat with me and told me all the horrific events that occurred in his life within that five-year span. As I was talking to him, I was trying to recall if I had seen any signs when we were children that would have predicted his present state. In the meantime, my son, who is a millennial ran through my house trying to find clothes for him and bagged up some can goods to give to him. When he presented it to my friend, my son was crying—horrified that anyone could live this way, and my son looked at me truly angry that I did not do more to help him. In that one act, my buddy saw the heaviness of his plight reflected in my son's eyes and he looked so ashamed. I never saw him again after that day.

This story was not an excuse of a purposeless and directionless generation. What I shared with you was the formation of Generation X skewed from the eyes of a Black woman who was fortunate to

have seen what a Black hero looks like. I was able to see through the veneer of most of the world's sociopathic paths and plots that caught and destroyed most of my friends and loved ones. The ones that survived are almost shell-shocked. I believe it was the intention of "the world" to destroy any imagery of the Black hero. It was the intention of "the world" to wipe out our family structures, our voices, our sages, our inheritances, and our sense of responsibility to our communities.

As it stands, my generation of Black women and men gave birth to millennials and they are pissed off at us. We left them without fathers, homes, structures, stability, and made them fend for themselves. They are so segregated and vulnerable that they are not prepared for a revolution. However, while millennials are looking at us, baby boomers, with disdain and cynicism, it is important to remember that on your heels is the Generation Z—your children and our grandchildren.

These babies do not see Black or white, Jew or Gentile, fat or skinny, pretty or ugly, male or female. They only see themselves—the generation of "selfies." They do not need to listen to you. They are watching you blame us. They do not need any sages; they have their iPhones and anything they need to know can be obtained from Siri and Google. I think I may have gone on a tangent, but it felt necessary as I cannot talk about my washing as a Black woman without addressing the life I have lived and the experiences I have, regarding Black folks. However, in reference to the question: How do you teach the world to properly wash Black women? You do not. You teach the Black woman to give her cloth to Jesus and allow Him to bathe her in empathy and truth. Empathy is the psychological identification with our vicarious experiencing of the feelings, thoughts, or attitudes of another. And just as we need empathy while generations commune with one another across time and experience, we need empathy to guide our understanding about where we came from so, we do not repeat it.

I do not think it would be beneficial for Black women to give the world instructions on how to properly wash us. This world gave us our stains. My strength and resilience are the result of my washing, not the antidote to my stains. Therefore, in my opinion, giving the world a cloth to wash us would be analogous to giving a sociopath a stick to beat us. It would only give the world another weapon to form against us. For this reason, I would like to give my advice to Black women directly so that she will be able to find the antidote to her individual stains.

BLACK WASHED | *A Collection of Essays, Poems, Dreams, and Letters Addressed to Black Folk*

My personal truth is the Holy Spirit through Jesus Christ. Only He can teach truth. He supernaturally protected me from some of the world's most horrific situations and events. I wish I could say that my savvy or intellect prevented me from not teetering into the plight of some of my friends and loved ones, but I cannot. All I did was accept the love and protection of a loving God, and for whatever reason, He saw fit to prevent me from facing some of those situations, and when I survived it, gave me the lens to be able to share this snapshot with you. It is the same God that can show Himself to this generation of youth that do not see the need to acknowledge Him—yet. It is the same God that can help this generation of Black women to forgive the generations of Black women before them, so we can wash together.

DENNIS MAURICE

Bad Lighting

A Poem Addressed to Black Folk

Bad Lighting

I came into the space bright.

Shining like new nickel.

Captivating shine is what I bring.

I have found my passion inside of deeply hidden, dim rooms, by offering my lightning and revival.

Until I was informed that

I was poorly lit,

Not equipped,

And incredibly insufficient to illuminate my own murky alley way—let alone somebody else's.

This is bad lighting. I had bad lighting.

I will never be content with insufficient radiance, so I decided to grab my piece of the sun.

I grabbed my sun share from the sky and took it everywhere I went.

I took my sun to the church, but they said God didn't want it…

I took my sun to my hood, but they said it distracted everyone.

I took my sun to my family and they said I was punishing them with my light.

I sat with my sun and figured it was all true… I am just insufferable, scantily ignited, poorly lit…

Nah, fuck that
I am the fire… I know I'm lit.

If I keep on shining eventually folk will receive my glow as I intend.

And even if they do not, my lumens will still grow like babies in ages of wombs hitherto.

I take my sun and mix it with the God alive in me and wrap our light around my dim body.

I layer Him meticulously over my sun.

This light is my generational wealth, a heritage of beauty-filled flames that are an honor to carry.

DENNIS MAURICE

Surely, all these dark, poorly lit, murky spaces had to see my glow.

But ain't nobody care about this shine, no matter how bright, they just turned me down…low.

In fact, now they called my light flamboyant.

Said I was only shining like this to make folk feel a way.

Gloomy, muddy souls told me I needed to find God, while I was dressed in Him.

Gloomy, muddy souls

told me

I needed to find God…

While I was dressed

in Him.

What do I to do with that?

I threw away my share of the sun…

I threw away the God living in me…

I threw away the beauty-filled flames gifted to me through ages of wombs hitherto.

Mortally dim I had to depend on whatever light I could find…

Lookin' at folk shine and envying what I could do with their fortune…

I was a turn-off, turned off.

Gifts from ages of wombs are now cursed—buried deeply beneath forgotten worth.

BLACK WASHED | *A Collection of Essays, Poems, Dreams, and Letters Addressed to Black Folk*

Everything Will Burn

A Short Addressed to Black Folk

DENNIS MAURICE

Everything Will Burn

> **Whether you fry it or boil it.**
> **If you leave it in the pot too long**
> **Everything will burn.**

Whether ya Auntie Black or anti-Black…
You are laying prostrate—flat—on soil that's been ganked and "bought" "again…"
Fry the cabbage so niggas can eat…
It can use a few clipped wings of a smoked-out bird… for flavor…
Or a little sugar… and while you at it…
Boil down your thoughts 'til they not yowns no more…
It gotta make you feel full being this empty…
If life ain't taught us nothing, it's taught us this…
You can hide ya money in the mattress and they'll still run up and take ya home…
Leave ya there…
It don't take much.
In the end they 'gon get there's and yowns, too…
The name of the game ain't familiar but niggas is playing it…
Pot calling the kettle rusted…
Too many years of ignored, unvarnished surfaces will destroy any pot and any kettle…
Long ways to go and a lot of dying and living behind us and we hope more to come…
Everything has to be remembered to be forgiven…
Will take no compromise—can't have my body or can't handle this muhfuckin' my mind…
Burn this bitch down through the core… not just for today but for everything before.

> **Whether you fry it or boil it.**
> **If you leave it in the pot too long**
> **Everything will burn.**

BLACK WASHED | *A Collection of Essays, Poems, Dreams, and Letters Addressed to Black Folk*

Church Punch

A Reflection Addressed to Black Folk

Church Punch

I grew up in South Philly and lived at church as a child. We attended a church that could seat 1,000 but had about 75 consistent members—Greater Mount Olive AME Church.

I learned so much every time I ran through those doors.

The most important thing I learned was the recipe for church punch.

Now, if you do not know about church punch then you probably have good control of your blood sugar, because this beautiful, blessed beverage will turn your sweat into simple syrup. Each batch is seasoned with an icy drum of homemade sweet tea, punch, and lemonade from a month of Sundays past.

The flavor can never be cloned, because about 10 church punch chefs done added their flair in each mix that came prior.

Church Punch is a refreshing Black classic; hand-stirred with a steady circular shoulder sweep that lifts every sweet granule to be dissolved into an uninterruptable recipe that creates a homeopathic liquor that rejects duplication. Ladled into an 8-ounce Styrofoam cup.

Yes, it is that deep.

It is generally escorted by baked or fried chicken, 7-UP cake, and tiny pastel mints & peanuts in round glass bowls on the crest of rectangle tables swathed in pale plastic slips.

We would guzzle that punch and it was like that surge through our divinely worn bodies was the offering and we were the collection plate.

God loves a cheerful giver, and that punch pours with praise.

Filled up.

Now there's energy to survive the guest preacher at second service.

This uniquely flavored tonic sweetened with histories and rituals depends on the love of *all* that mixed batches before it was poured into my 8-ounce Styrofoam cup.

Many of the hands and unspoken recipes are now gone.

I am glad I savored it then, because I can't recreate it now.

BLACK WASHED | *A Collection of Essays, Poems, Dreams, and Letters Addressed to Black Folk*

LYNCHING *Six*
LANGUAGE

"Between 1882 and 1967, 200 bills were presented before congress to outlaw lynching. Additionally, seven presidents urged congress to end the practice. Each time these efforts were rejected by Congress and lynching continued unabated and unpunished. It was not until 2005 that the U.S. Senate offered an apology for what it termed "domestic terrorism" mostly against Black people."

- Joy DeGruy, PhD
Post Traumatic Slave Syndrome: America's Legacy of Enduring Injury and Healing

The Emmett Till Anti-Lynching Act was introduced by Rep. Bobby Lee Rush of Illinois on January 3, 2019 and has yet to be approved by the Senate as of January 3, 2021. Lynching has been challenged for 139 years and this form of terror has a history of targeting Black, Indigenous, and Mexican folk for at least 191 years. This is America and white terrorism is as American as confederate flags, theft of land, collusion, and apple pies cooling on windowsills. And this Devil ain't got no new tricks.

Welcome to Chapter six: Lynching Language—Foreword Author: Stephanie D. Keene.

Six

Foreword Author

Stephanie D. Keene

Stephanie D. Keene is a Philadelphia-based writer, educator, and creator. She owns Incense, Trap, & Yoga, an apparel line that promotes a culture of justice. Her other justice work focuses on prison and police abolition. A proud graduate of the first HBCU, Lincoln University (PA), she is working for the freedom of all people.

Me, too, Sis…

Stephanie D. Keene

BLACK WASHED | *A Collection of Essays, Poems, Dreams, and Letters Addressed to Black Folk*

"I thought I was going to harm… the movement."

Me, too, sis.

In the spring of 2014, I met a charismatic leader and activist at the forefront of the movement for criminal justice reform in America. For almost four years I have been trying to forget him.

I was working for a domestic violence program in Philadelphia and had begun teaching workshops on the subject inside a women's correctional facility. Working with those women changed my life in ways I could not have imagined. Ways that are particularly resonant as I find the voice to write this.

As a result of my work with the women in the correctional facility, my program director sent me and a few colleagues to a local symposium about the impact of the prison industrial complex. Attendees and panelists included activists, educators, people who were formerly incarcerated, law enforcement staff, artists, and social workers. The keynote speaker for the event was a handsome Black man in his early 40s, dressed meticulously in a tailored suit, and finished with expensive dental work. He spoke of the importance of prioritizing the voices of people who have been directly impacted by the criminal legal system. He observed that "those closest to the problem are closest to the solution but furthest from resources and power." Finally, he shared his own story, strategically saving the reveal of his past incarceration until the exact moment the audience was captivated by his charm, his intellect, and his command of the stage.

He was good at this.
He knew it.

And he made sure to humbly point out that these traits do not make him exceptional as a formerly incarcerated person; that many people who have spent time in this country's prisons and jails are brilliant and talented and capable.

I did not actually meet Davis* after his speech. Instead, I went to another room for a workshop and continued to tweet some of the highlights of the day, using the organizers' hashtags for the event. That evening I received a tweet from him. I had followed him and thought that he had read my tweets and realized I had been at the event. Later he would tell me that too many people had followed him that day for him to have noticed individual profiles. Instead, he had noticed me in the crowd during his speech and later searched the hashtags for the event until he found me. I was flattered.

He was good at this.

DENNIS MAURICE

He Knew it.

We moved our conversation to private Twitter messages. We exchanged pleasantries about the event itself and talked about prison activism. We playfully engaged in standard Philly vs. New York City banter. He asked about my interest in the movement. I asked about his next steps with his new organization. He eventually asked for my number. We moved our conversation to a phone call. He told me he would be in Philly again within the week and asked to take me to lunch. I was not available. He impishly pouted and insisted that this meant I had to come to Harlem for dinner soon.

A few weeks and many conversations later, I drove to Harlem. I got lost as I approached his neighborhood. He called me and was noticeably agitated. I wrote it off as the New Yorker in him. When I finally arrived, he got into the passenger seat of my car and directed me to the parking garage where he kept his car. He gave me his spot, and we got into his car to go to dinner at a soul food restaurant in his rapidly gentrifying neighborhood. The evening was pleasant. There were flashes of what I now believe to be narcissism. However, whenever he read alarm on my face, he flashed his $50K smile and transitioned into jokes and more banter.

He was good at this.
He knew it.

We dated for just a few months. He asked me if I would be willing to meet his 4-year-old son. I suggested we wait until we had known each other longer. He agreed and said that his "crazy" ex, the child's mother, would probably respond to that better.

We continued to meet over long weekends and planned breaks. He never came to Philly; I always went to him. The nonprofit he started did not have a board yet, and he was working from his Harlem apartment doing everything from fundraising to public relations. We would hang out between conference calls and walk to neighborhood spots for lunch. He asked me if I would consider moving to New York and working for the organization. "Imagine how powerful we could be together," he would say. I never responded directly.

Eventually, he suggested that we share our electronic calendars with each other to make arranging our time together easier. Part of me thought he wanted to prove how busy and important he was, but most of me thought it was a sweet gesture. One day, I went to check his calendar to plan for a visit, and there was an entry that read "Family trip to purchase wedding bands." He had accepted the invitation. I did an internet search for the name of the person who had created the event. She had a blog where she mentioned Davis* as her husband and referenced their 4-year-old son together. Upset but not all that confused, I sent him a short text, something along the lines of "So apparently you're married. Great. We're done here." In responding, he practically refused to address the issue. He only wanted to know if I was still driving up that weekend. It was like a text version of that $50K smile. When I refused, he insisted that the calendar entry was a "bad joke" from his "crazy ex." When I insisted that I was done with our budding relationship, he responded: "Drop dead, bitch."

What followed for the next 6 months were periodic texts from him telling me about how I had ruined everything: us, **the movement**, the potential of his organization, the summer he could've enjoyed. He also added insults about my self-worth and sexuality, and accusations about my intentions and motives. He never acknowledged his marriage, his lies, or his threats, which were just thinly veiled enough not to be illegal. Looking back, I often wonder if my work in the field of domestic violence was a welcomed challenge for him. But, then again, that would require an acknowledgment on his part and that his behavior was abusive. I stopped responding after the first few weeks. Eventually, he stopped texting.

He never went away though. In the fall of the following year, I began working for a prison education organization. On my first day, we were planning a conference celebrating the organization's upcoming anniversary. We were discussing potential keynote speakers, and someone suggested Davis*. I stopped breathing. I began to silently identify and name objects in the room, a tactic I use to prevent anxiety attacks. The meeting ended with folks agreeing that we should invite him. I could not speak.

Months later (before any invitations went out), I confided in an older male colleague about my experience, including that I had been too ashamed and afraid to tell the group. He knew Davis* casually and said "I'm not surprised. I'll handle it." The invitation did not go out.

For the duration of my employment with that organization, I spent a lot of time wondering if Davis* would be present at events I was obligated to attend. I would ask other colleagues to go in my stead when Davis* was on the program, without explaining why I wouldn't/could not go. When I did go, I vigilantly surveyed the room for the exits, just in case he showed up. By then I did not fear as much for my physical safety. Not because I trusted him, but because I figured his care for his reputation would not allow him to act out in public spaces. My fear was for my emotional well-being. Could I even breathe with him in the room?

Davis* would go on to give national TV interviews and appear in groundbreaking films about incarceration in America. He founded a successful movement to close a notorious jail in the state of New York. He received honors and awards as an advocate for human rights.

He was good at this.

And he was unavoidable in the work that I now knew was a critical piece of my calling.

DENNIS MAURICE

Besides family and a few close friends, nobody knew about my experience with this man. This leader in the community. This voice. Few knew how I'd cringe when I would stumble upon him on TV or a popular podcast. How I prepared myself to encounter him in critically acclaimed films. How I hadn't been able to visit Harlem since that spring.

I considered speaking out a few times. But I struggled. I didn't know if it would matter. And I couldn't quite name what I had been through. I hadn't been sexually assaulted. I hadn't been physically abused. I had the language of "emotional abuse," but even that didn't feel like… enough. What I felt was more convoluted than that. There was this element of feeling terrorized within the spaces in which I needed to be present in order to do what was necessary and just.

Aside from struggling with the words, I struggled with wanting to maintain my privacy. To not have my name attached in any way to this man and his behavior. And to not have his behavior attached in any way to the movement. We were both doing important work, and I didn't want something so messy to detract from that. And I didn't want people to be able to point at him and make sweeping generalizations about currently and formerly incarcerated people, many of whom I love and admire. I decided to remain quiet. For myself, for the movement, for the people we were all collectively trying to create space and justice for.

And then I heard whispers that he'd resigned from the organization he had founded. No details were offered. But my spirit shifted. I knew. A few days later, a friend who I'd confided in showed me an article in the New York Times. Davis* had been accused of "sexual misconduct" by at least 3 former employees, one of whom had been paid $25,000 for her silence (she later decided to breach the agreement to stand in solidarity with the other two women). She said she hadn't spoken out before because, "I thought I was going to harm quote, unquote the movement." I decided to speak.

My story isn't the same as these women's stories. But it's related. And it's relevant. And telling. And justice requires, for me at least, that I share my piece of the story.

Too often, Black women and femmes in social justice movements are given this false dichotomy of choosing between ideals: Are we down for "the cause," or are we down for making sure activist spaces are safe for everyone who shows up? I decided I'm tired of choosing.

This is the work of washing Black women—of removing the layers of disrespect and disregard with which the world desecrates us at every turn. We wash Black women by standing up for (and with) Black women.

BLACK WASHED | *A Collection of Essays, Poems, Dreams, and Letters Addressed to Black Folk*

"Those closest to the problem are closest to the solution but furthest from resources and power." Women who are harmed by powerful men within social justice movements are often rendered powerless. But we are our own resources. Our collective voices and our willingness to tell our stories create a reckoning that cannot be ignored.

What good is a movement if its people are immobilized?

We have begun to speak. And we will not stop.

>*Name has been changed, not to protect the subject, but to give the author peace and agency.
[An earlier edit of this piece first appeared on Medium.com.]

DENNIS MAURICE

Vertigo

A Poem Addressed to Black Folk who have been forced to hold their tongues while enduring white terror.

BLACK WASHED | *A Collection of Essays, Poems, Dreams, and Letters Addressed to Black Folk*

Vertigo

VERTIGO [vur-ti-goh] NOUN:

a dizzying sensation of
tilting within stable surroundings

or of

being in tilting or spinning surroundings.

Sometimes, in the stillness of life I taste an uproar in my spirit; stirring up sour truths that boil inside of me.
Sour.
Sourness that lives in the not-so-hidden spaces of my survival.

Silent Screams.
Silent screams that only I can hear, shouting for relief—this is lonely pain.

This spiritual acid burns through my cartilage, deteriorating these seemingly stable bones.

Hazardous.
Hazardous liquid running through my veins; flooding *this side of soil* like a river filled with burning acid. Acid that races through me, wilting my fractured bones, corrupting my balance.

Scared.
This is deep, maniacal, deliberate pain.

Vertigo.
I cannot stand straight with weak bones.

I smile.
I smile with clenched teeth to protect you from this lava I have stored.

I feel like a masochist.
My interior burns with a smile.
I am tilting, uncontrolled, and I know eventually I will fall.

I feel full grown and primitive, concurrently
While I look still, no one can see how this sour acid burns through my internal fortress.

DENNIS MAURICE

I pray.
I pray for the power to release this revolting vitriol that holds a hostel in me;
have it pass through my throat and out my mouth.

I need to taste it leaving my body.
Let it pass through my invented smile.

I pray.
I pray that it burns through every tooth in my mouth, relieving me of this burning, painful truth behind this nasty manufactured simper.

I welcome this vomit.
I am ready for this relief—I am living for it and I am dying without it.
I am straightening my back and standing up in the face of this dizzying sensation.

For protection, I will stand still like God's ground and keep this bubbling at bay.

I hope to.
I got to.
I will…
rebuild these weak bones.

BLACK WASHED | *A Collection of Essays, Poems, Dreams, and Letters Addressed to Black Folk*

Lynching Language

An Introspective Thesis Addressed to Black Folk

Lynching Language

"I was going to die, sooner or later, whether or not I had even spoken myself. My silences had not protected me. Your silences will not protect you... What are the words you do not yet have? What are the tyrannies you swallow day by day and attempt to make your own, until you will sicken and die of them, still in silence? We have been socialized to respect fear more than our own need for language."

-Audre Lorde

I learned Black words first.

Growing in a Black body is an honor. Black bodies have been maligned, defiled, lynched, appropriated, and stolen, but Black minds existed before and have evolved despite it all. Our minds allow us to turn gumbo into language and language into revolution. Lorde's quote invites us into the idea that unused language and the inability to critique the condition of many things is a miscarriage of the words we need to give birth to the humane, complex story of us. Our story's genesis is not the shell of a Black body, but the journey of a Black mind. And within our Black minds lives our ability to articulate where our human experience—absent of white things—rambles with untamed passion.

I learned Black words first. **Then I learned to swallow them whole.**

Around 2001 while studying literature and philosophy in college, I began to study and critique how people expressed themselves. Throughout my analysis, I was amazed that folk from Baltimore did not recognize they had an accent. With confidence and trembles of joy in their tone they said things like hut dug (hot dog) and it seemed impossible that they had not yet recognized the glaring distinction in their dialect. Accents are generally defined by one's pronunciation of words. And pronunciation of words is generally characteristic of one's environment. However, every time I heard folk with a strong Black, Baltimore accent I developed bias of what I thought about them.

The ways they shared their language, and how they told their story, was challenging for me. I constructed a problem with how their environment supported their voice and sought ways to separate my voice from theirs. My dislike grew into invented suggestions about Baltimore folk and their devolving humanities. Years later I struggled with my disdain.

Was it me or is it them?

Plot twist: It was me.

BLACK WASHED | *A Collection of Essays, Poems, Dreams, and Letters Addressed to Black Folk*

I lynched their tongues with every rolled eye, unseen wince, and pessimistic descriptor. Undeniably, I informed my positions in a vacuum of anti-Blackness that directed me to dig for soot in their never-ending wells, because they were out of the uniform of my prejudice and particularity.

I chose violence. I chose insecurity. I chose to make myself feel better, bolder, appropriately Blacker by criticizing the tongue they knew with the tongue I found. By conflating their value with their dialectal style, solely, I welcomed misunderstanding them. *them… them*. us. I very easily denied them and me access to humanity and Blackness through my refusal to hear any of their melodies.

I learned Black words first. Then I learned to swallowed them whole. **Then I learned to swallow the people who dared to utter those Black words again.**

April 19, 2015, Freddie Carlos Gray, Jr. is murdered by the Baltimore Police. Black Baltimore rises and reminds us that everything will burn. The news was filled with countless Back folk sharing a new song. I went to work the next day at a well-meaning, white-led nonprofit and a group of people commented on the Black, Baltimore accents they heard on the news, noting that they had never heard their style of speech. I was immediately offended. How dare these low-minded folks reduce my folk to dialect and accents amid them fighting for their lives. I could not understand how they deconstructed their humanity into phrasing and cadence; never listening to the message in their language. They were lynching their language. Just like I did. Except now I see clearly that I lynched three native tongues—theirs, mine, and ours.

And there it is. The reminder. The answer. The story. The end.

I learned Black words first. Then I learned to swallowed them whole. Then I learned to swallow the people who dared to utter those Black words again. **Then I re-learned Black words.**

DENNIS MAURICE

Black Lemons

A Poem Addressed to Black Folk

BLACK WASHED | *A Collection of Essays, Poems, Dreams, and Letters Addressed to Black Folk*

Black Lemons

Our death is not our nativity.

We came before Columbus and before Pilgrims and before Jim Crow.

Black life does not begin when crooked white and blue knees crush Black windpipes.

Black life does not begin when militarized overseers spray 32 rounds of 'wanton endangered' ammunition into the wrong Black home and the wrong Black woman.

Black life does not begin when a racist vigilante kills a 16-year-old Black boy for fear that he may be a 16-year-old Black boy.

Black death is not a Black nativity.

Black life began when we used chicken bones as teething rings and Black girls sang *"Hey DJ won't ya play that song? Keep ya foot in all day long…"* while jumping double dutch.

Black life began with the first sting of alcohol after your barber rubbed down your neck and it continued when we sharpened already pointy pencils in the front of class to show off fresh cuts.

Black life began snapping string bean ends into paper bags to earn your keep.

Black life began with bow ties and bumped bangs on Easter Sunday.

Black life began with cousins that were like siblings sharing twin beds with grandma for weekends.

Black life began with glass bowls & matching ladles filled with red punch and floating fruit for house party celebrations.

Black life began with dreams of fish and Ginger Ale as our first prescription.

DENNIS MAURICE

Our death is not our nativity.

We are powerful in our stillness.

We are alive in our slumber.

We exist outside of news cycles.

We mattered before hashtags.

We had voices before Twitter.

We had a song before the Blues…

And Gospel…

And Jazz…

And Motown…

And R&B

And Rappers' Delight.

We had culture before Maafa.

We had bodies before they stole them.

We have life with or without you…

Like Jesus our story does not begin when they nail us, and we are reborn.

We are designed with thread that crafts our du-rag, headwrap, and white tee.

Our death will never be our nativity.

BLACK WASHED | *A Collection of Essays, Poems, Dreams, and Letters Addressed to Black Folk*

REST WITHOUT COMPROMISE

Seven

"They in their cruel traps, and we in ours,
Survey each other's rage, and pass the hours
Commiserating each the other's woe,
To mitigate his own pain's fiery glow.
Man could but little proffer in exchange
Save that his cages have a larger range.
That lion with his lordly, untamed heart
Has in some man his human counterpart,
Some lofty soul in dreams and visions wrapped,
But in the stifling flesh securely trapped…"
   Countee Cullen,
   An excerpt of "Thoughts in a Zoo"
   My Soul's High Song: The Collected Writings of Countee Cullen (© 1991)

Welcome to Chapter seven: Rest Without Compromise—Foreword Author: TheeAmazingGrace.

Seven

Foreword Author

TheeAmazingGrace (Gracie Berry)

Gracie Berry is a Black, queer, cis-woman, community root-healer, freelance creative, and womanist. As a griot, she finds it important to share life from an Afro-diasporic experience before any of the margins. Gracie is a proud matrilineal descendant from the Mende People in Sierra Leone, born in West Philadelphia. An alumnus of Lincoln University of Pennsylvania, the nation's first degree granting HBCU, Gracie is the embodiment of breaking generational curses, being the first on her mother's side to graduate from college.

She is the owner of GirlrillaVintage, an Afrikan Roots and empowerment organization. Through her company she is sharing Afrikan cultural diasporic content, events, and perspectives through offerings of education, expressive arts, spirituality, vintage aesthetic, workshops, etc. All of Gracie's offerings serve as tools to engage people of Afrikan descent in becoming more aware of their inherent birth right to their blood culture and identity, no matter how they were born into it.

DENNIS MAURICE

Save Some Savin' for Yourself

TheeAmazingGrace (Gracie Berry)

BLACK WASHED | *A Collection of Essays, Poems, Dreams, and Letters Addressed to Black Folk*

I mean this from my heart chakra, a spiritual, light-being having a human experience. To wash this Black woman properly is a simple task, really.

You must first save your own life.

No matter how deep, how invested, how much I want to save you, need to save you, or try to convince my actions into saving you, I can never save you.

You must save your own life.

You must be the center of your own healing. No matter how much I cherish you—Stay strong for you. Worship each part of you.

You must save your own life.

However, we can still coexist—just like our bodies in the rain. Don't you know that the rain is our prodigy? I bow my head to worship the droplets. Don't you know that our hearts become clean when we cry? Lest we forget we were babies born crying—wet with rain we call tears. Wailing is a gift I give to myself. I welcome the wailing mantra. Shedding tears is one of my healing rituals. I listen to the sounds my cries make. I react by crying louder, crying harder, crying with purpose. I ignite my ancestral alter (literally).

The candle.
The sage.
The pictures.
Our memories.

A damn good cry. I intuit the sounds leaving my throat chakra. My grief leaves my root chakra. My grief always gives birth to healing.

This is how I save my own life.

I recall, the one-time my mother washed me with the love and kindness she had left. During a time when our only way of life was plagued by her crack addiction, abandonment, life threatening beatings, fear, and finding new ways to walk on eggshells. She had a combined birthday party to celebrate my 7th year and my younger brother's 4th year, one week apart. The life size bag of popcorn from Murray's Market, a homemade cake, my dearest cousins, aunties and uncles, the sodas, candy, music from the component set, the balloons, dancing, all of it washed my heart in a way. But it was the way she loved on me that day, the safety she gave me that day, made a big ole fuss over me, the kindness in her eyes, sweet talk in her voice (the way she called me Grace face), the way her hands moved with purpose to fry the chicken, and how generous she was with my favorite sweet relish in the potato salad—the pain I had become so accustomed to, was being washed out of my bones. My mama washed me, in a way, and that day will fill me for life.

I remember the first time I learned to wash myself clean and to lay my burdens out to dry. It was deep in the summer and I was about 10 years old. I had two breast buds forming that felt like those irritating, hard, shiny, pimples on the nose. They were painful little rocks and that ugly, white, lace bra was the worse, especially the straps. We slid across the hot, sticky, leather car seats, me, grandma, uncle, and Lynn. We were going to pay our respects to my birth father's mother who passed away. My uncle reached over to fasten his seat belt and inadvertently elbowed my right breast bud, I whimpered like a wounded dog, but not for too long. Uncle told me told me that he didn't mean to hit my little "mosquito bite" and that he was sorry. He bullied me into fixing my face 'cause he didn't want me to mess up my pretty dress, he said. Everyone laughed at me. I swallowed the phantom lump in my throat, wiped my tears, and looked straight ahead.

We arrived at the church, the moment they were carrying the casket that held the body of my father's mother (at least that's what grandma said). I didn't choose to swallow the phantom lump in my throat this time. I wailed so hard and loud that I fell to my knees, people stared at me. Strangely, I couldn't stop sobbing. I couldn't stop crying for a lady I never knew. I didn't care about being punished. I think I cried for an hour.

I washed myself that day by choosing not to be silent about my pain.
I haven't been silent about it ever since.

I gave my daddy permission to wash me, too, with ease and compassion. I wanted to jump out of my skin, but instead I jumped into his arms, wiping snot and tears all over his suit jacket. I allowed him to comfort me during my most vulnerable time. He shared the sweetest stories about my hazel eyed grandmother and how I reminded him of her sweet spirit. This was the moment he told me that our ancestors never leave us, so I could talk to her whenever I wanted. It was a miracle how much better I felt after all of that.

Black wash is real.
Healing Black is real.
It's changed my entire life.

BLACK WASHED | *A Collection of Essays, Poems, Dreams, and Letters Addressed to Black Folk*

Requiem

A Dream Addressed to Black Folk

Requiem

I celebrate Black life because…

Every celebration of Black living

Is a requiem for the things that tried to kill us.

I celebrate Black things not just because of my pride

Though I am embellished with plenty…

I celebrate Black things in the hope that anti-Black things die painfully.

I celebrate Black things in preparation of a world that values humanity principally.

I celebrate Black things in the hope that they construct monuments on green grass, between Black hands and red clay.

I celebrate Black things because we created a life on land we cannot truly call home.

I will become a celebration…

I will become a celebration that honors the strata of Black tongues and touch.

I will become a celebration that is covered in Black deities.

I will become a celebration that exists in warm spaces, not cold blood.

I will become a celebration that is Black like us.

I will become a celebration in front of the caskets of everything that tried to kill us.

No Bone

A Poem Addressed to Black Folk who are alive in fat bodies in a fatphobic world.

No Bone

Was I created with no bone?

Loving cheek pinches transform into prefiguring my life's quality based on form and figure.

There're girls out there that like a big boy…

Who you tryna convince?

And I don't want her… like that.

…but that story might ignite a new trigger.

Am I only skin, flesh, fat, and nigga?

To you.

Unable to move, manage, or motivate…

My body, heaviness, or self

Via your appraisal.

Was I created with no bone?

Coming into era, in a fat, Black body, stamped with tales of sweet crystals sent to kill me…

And all I love.

A life bastardized and reduced to big arms that must be fortified by cake batter…

No mind.

No soul.

No bone.

BLACK WASHED | *A Collection of Essays, Poems, Dreams, and Letters Addressed to Black Folk*

Am I just skin, flesh, fat, and nigga?

To you.

Where did you place my mind when you exchanged my life for a body…

hallow and full,

no questions?

just like that?

Did you at least place my soul in a safe space, so you can find it again when you realize I am full…?

And not just full figured?

Did you throw my bones in the ocean to lay with ancestors seen as only skin, flesh, and nigga?

Where did you place me when you chose to see my body and disregard my humanity?

Am I just skin, flesh, fat, and nigga?

To you.

Was I born into this fetish or adopted?

Existing in a world that ejaculates bad news on my body for kinks is exhausting.

I am more than just skin, flesh, fat, and nigga.

To me.

I am of

chunky mind…

plump soul…

big bone.

DENNIS MAURICE

BLACK AS CAIN
Eight

'Twas mercy brought me from my *Pagan* land,
Taught my benighted soul to understand
That there's a God, that there's a *Saviour* too:
Once I redemption neither sought nor knew.
Some view our sable race with scornful eye,
"Their colour is a diabolic die."
Remember, *Christians*, *Negros*, black as *Cain*,
May be refin'd, and join th' angelic train.

- Phillis Wheatley
One Being Brought from Africa to America

Welcome to Chapter eight: Black as Cain—Foreword Author: Leonia Johnson.

BLACK WASHED | *A Collection of Essays, Poems, Dreams, and Letters Addressed to Black Folk*

Eight

Black Woman Foreword Author

Leonia Johnson

Leonia Johnson is a proud Philadelphia native, an Artist, Community Leader/Activist, and Christian Therapist. She attended Lincoln University in Pennsylvania, where she received a Bachelor of Science in Psychology and in 2011, Leonia received a Master of Science degree in Christian Counseling from Cairn University.

Throughout her career she has served in various settings, implementing biblical practices to serve humanity at large. From working with "At Risk-Youth," to helping dual diagnosed individuals and returning citizens within the justice system, Leonia knows her passion and calling is to see the gospel affect change in society.

Leonia believes in living out missions and evangelism in everyday life (as is evident in Col 3:17 and Mt 28:18-20). She loves to travel and believes that everywhere that her feet are blessed to explore is a mission field. In her travels, Leonia has visited various places in North America, West Africa, and Europe with the hopes of distinguishing Christianity from Western Culture and seeing the gospel bring unity while knowing that Christ alone can bring peace.

She is a proud "Philly Jawn" that loves her niece, Peyton, all melanated people, The Philadelphia Eagles, and working with youth and young adults from various backgrounds. Leonia is active within her community and for 15 years continues to serve as one of the youngest Block Captains the City of Philadelphia.

One of her aims in working with youth is to equip the nation's future leaders with a biblical world view, assist with discipleship and display how the gospel can be culturally relevant while bringing practical help, healing, and unity to all who believe.

A Haiku:
God Did it.

Leonia Johnson

DENNIS MAURICE

our hue is not filth
we don't need you to clean us
God did and does that

BLACK WASHED | *A Collection of Essays, Poems, Dreams, and Letters Addressed to Black Folk*

A 3-Tier Cake

A Letter Addressed to Black Queer Folk
(Originally written for April & Janine)

DENNIS MAURICE

A 3-Tier Cake

10/05/2018

Dear April & Janine:

Picture it, Philly 1989, I am about 7 years old attending my first wedding—excited, determined to see how love works. I had seen figurines with white gowns and white faces on perfectly iced three-tier cakes, but I knew love had more to offer. Because even though I had only seen white brides and grooms on cakes I knew that black brides and grooms existed. And although I had only seen men and women as couples, I had an idea that more love than that existed. At 7-years-old I knew that the love I had seen was not synonymous with the love I desired or should expect.

When I think about the identities and spectrums of love I recognize it is layered, woven together with threads perfectly placed to connect two pieces of fabric that need each other to form a more perfect garment. The fabrics have sameness and difference, yet all function with the same purpose.

So, picture it, Philly 2018—I am in my 30s and I am at my first wedding that honors the resilient love of two amazing Black women. And just like my 7-year-old self I am excited and determined to see how this love works. I am watching every interaction and glance and deepening my understanding of love by watching your display, today. This is nothing like the white bride and groom figurines on three-tier cakes I had seen growing up. Yet, it is still love. This is *still* love.

What I know for sure is that there is God, peace, stillness, admiration, adoration, and living water in any space between folks that welcomes the beauty of love. Picture it, Philly October 5, 2018—and we experience the love of God through Black women on a three-tier cake. Amen.

Unarguably,

Dennis

BLACK WASHED | *A Collection of Essays, Poems, Dreams, and Letters Addressed to Black Folk*

Black & Empty

A Letter Addressed to Black Folk

Black & Empty

To Whom it May Resonate:

I am writing to you about empty Black folk. Growing up in South Philly I was impressed by the larger-than-life personalities living in our ordinary hood. I found everyone interesting and I would write stories about them when I was alone. I created fables about what I believed they were like when nobody was watching. They were the stars in my stories. I wrote about what life through the eyes of a child, reaching for existence and survival, looked like. There were also supporting identities that were comical, but not substantive, to me. We called them crackheads, pipers, winos, and other pejoratives and defined them by the ways they coped with life and not by their lives.

There was a woman named Tammi* and she was active. She walked fast, talked fast, and had a hustle in her spirit and a product to pitch. When she walked down my grandmother's block we would yell, "Hey Tammi!!!" and she would come back with a hilarious one-liner like, "Just getting finer by the day, wouldn't you say?" and then folk would say, "I know that's right, Tammi! That girl just as crazy!" To me, Tammi was a comedienne. She offered light and oxygen into the spaces she entered. Unfortunately, much of Tammi's life was unknown and never questioned. She had a personal relationship with drugs, and many defined her by that union. One day, Tammi walked on the block with measured speed, controlled language, and nothing to sell. We yelled, "Hey Tammi!!!" and she responded deliberately, "How y'all doing? Hey Ms. Lue. Hey Ms. Rosa." and continued to go about her day. Folk began to talk about how she was getting clean. They said she was leaving that mess behind. I was enamored. How can these two people live in one body? I was captivated by her ability to exist in multiple sensibilities. She was now interesting and transitioned from comic relief to the star of the stories I wrote about life around 7th Street.

From then on, I would watch Tammi closely and with intrigue. Now, she was telling everyone about her dreams, goals, and newfound spiritual life. Everyone supported it and her with appropriate ovation, yet this reworking of her was much more mundane. Every now and again someone would say "You just getting finer by the day, Tammi…" and she would respond "Oh y'all remember that? I was deep in my mess back then…" Her mood changed and soon when folk saw the new Tammi, they had less conversation for her, and she reciprocated their vibe accordingly.

BLACK WASHED | *A Collection of Essays, Poems, Dreams, and Letters Addressed to Black Folk*

Before this time Tammi had been a caricature of a life, a hyperbolic mess of witty revivals and survival skills. I never saw her as human, or humane, or with humanity. I saw her as wit and charm and headwraps and gelled edges and big sunglasses and tank tops and maroon nails that were never chipped, in a tall, slender frame. She was reduced until her womanhood, mindset, and soul were boiled down from living water to humidity.

Years later I heard that Tammi passed away. A mix of domestic abuse and addiction were labeled as the cause. Someone said, "Well at least she ain't in pain no more." I was puzzled. I did not understand that storing pain created expressions, and habits, and issues, and decisions, and moods. I saw her as a soul ready to receive the world, but; in fact, she was too full to accept anything more. I began to wonder what Tammi's life would have been like if she had some room—a little emptiness. What would a Black and empty Tammi do, or say, or wear, or share, or be? Is she funny? Is she nice? Does she even live around here?

The idea of having enough room to create refined realities that do not have a foundation of pain beneath them is an honor. I wish and dream and hope for multitudes of Black folk with empty space. Black folk with enough space for gifts, living deep inside, to be freed to roam the world and utilized and materialized in ways we define. I pray for empty Black folk that do not have to store pain to keep still. I dream of Black lives consumed with unleashing enthusiastic dreams with no barriers. I hope one day we will all be Black and empty. I share this in remembrance of Tammi*.

Earnestly,

Dennis

*Name changed out of respect.

DEEPLY HOOD *Nine*

"I never saw her put eggs and cornmeal in it…"

A pint of milk, salt, pepper, Lawry's®, a few dashes of hot sauce, whiting—put it in a bowl. BOOM

Put some foil over the bowl and let that fish sit in it for half-hour in the refrigerator. BOP.

Get the bowl and drop a piece of fish into a paper bag with seasoned flour in it and shake. BANG

Put that coated fish in a cast iron filled with grease, fire on medium-high & cook 'til golden. BONG

Wait why the flour not sticking? It doesn't even look crunchy… Here she come…

"What you do to that fish?" "You ain't got cornmeal in the flour bag!!" "How many eggs put in?"

I know how to fry fish (I just never saw them use no eggs or cornmeal).

Go to Woods and get some wings—fried hard—ain't nobody eating that fish. BLOOP

Four wings fried hard—a hood classic. My next batch of fish gon' be a hood classic, too.

Welcome to Chapter nine: Deeply Hood—Foreword Author: Paula Ogden-Artwell.

BLACK WASHED | *A Collection of Essays, Poems, Dreams, and Letters Addressed to Black Folk*

Nine

Black Woman Foreword Author

Paula Ogden-Artwell

Born in South Philadelphia, Paula Ogden-Artwell is a wife, mother, teacher, and woman of God who aims to support, uplift, and inspire anyone in any way she can.

While Paula has been a mother to many through the joy of teaching for 17 years, she is also a dynamic and passionate mother of a beautiful and vibrant 4-year-old, Graysen.

Paula's marriage, among many other things in her life, is a testament to her faith in God. Paula's husband, Blake, has been one of her biggest and most cherished blessings.

Paula attended South Philadelphia High School, and later graduated from Lincoln University of Pennsylvania. She went on to receive her master's degree in Education from LaSalle University in Philadelphia. Paula has taught and worked with students between 2 - 18 years of age.

Paula has had a multifaceted life and holds near and dear to her, the relationships, and friendships that she has developed along the way. She always challenges the notion of keeping a "small circle" because she has acquired so many friends who are now part of her family.

A Collection:
Do Not Bleach, Do Not Dry Clean
Wash with Like Colors…
Gentle Cycle
Hand Wash Only

Paula Ogden-Artwell

DENNIS MAURICE

Do Not Bleach, Do Not Dry Clean.

To wash a Black woman, you must first examine her scars
The reason she is tarnished
the source of all her guards.

To wash a Black woman
you must locate her pain
inspect the dirt thrown on her name
grain by grain

To wash a Black woman
You must uncover every bruise
investigate where they came from and what she had to lose.

To wash a Black woman
examine her scars

To wash her thoroughly
determine the source of her guards.

Wash with Like Colors…

My girlfriends,

As we wash each other…I thank you. Washing a Black woman requires strength—elbow grease if you will. We stick together, have tough conversations, and we do not judge. When we DO judge…it is in LOVE and we handle it with laughter.

MY girls…**Y'all** wash me with open arms.
Y'all wash me with transparency.
Y'all wash me with words.
Y'all wash me…with prayer.

DENNIS MAURICE

Gentle Cycle

My husband,

Where does the cycle begin...and where does it end? You have tirelessly washed me of my past because you choose to forget and disregard it. You washed the scars and bruises from other men with love and understanding. You sewed up open wounds left from past relationships. You have stitched up insecurities. You have repaired and polished broken windows...the broken windows that used to help me look out into the life I thought I would never have. You not only repaired those windows, but you opened them and let fresh air inside. Fresh air that is the life I believed I could not have... determined I wasn't worthy of… the life I thought I missed out on. There are so many ways that you wash me, my love; I could never capture them all.

BLACK WASHED | *A Collection of Essays, Poems, Dreams, and Letters Addressed to Black Folk*

Hand Wash Only

My God,
My Father,
My Lord,

You have washed me in a way that no one on this earth could. God you washed my MIND. You washed my mind with your holy word. You have washed my heart with your presence. You have washed my spirit with your love. I could go on forever...Father....but I will say this: one of the most precious ways that you have washed me is with the people that you have placed in my life. The most important way that you have washed me is with your sacrifice. I love you Lord and Savior. It is because of You that I can say I'm clean.

Carnal Hymns

A Note Addressed to Black Folk forced to repress their sexual vibrations because we were taught that love for God meant our bodies had to be hidden, hated, and harmful.

Carnal Hymns

I can't wait for the day to let out a free, Black moan.

I mitigate my love for intimacy, sexual enthusiasm, and honest community
because it may hurt the image of sanitized Blackness that only believes in
nuclear families and heteronormative, ring bound unions,
but has no imagination for heauxs like me.

Shame stones thrown at my body and on my name because you chose to focus on my carnal fame.
I love who I am, and I like sharing, too.
I respect my body and I like a good consensual choking, too.
I will have long-term partners and fuck buddies, too.
You may not understand, but I ain't fuckin' you.
I used to be ashamed of my heaux fun until I recognized that a great many been one.
Still one.

Wailing in this sanctuary with heauxs like me on every pew.
And we all know that our pussy, and bussy, and dicks, and strap-ons are carnivals not museums.
We thank ancestors and deities for full, sacrosanct lives that include sexual texture.
Ain't no immaculate conception over here, folk are fucking and I mean that without conjecture.
I am not advocating for immorality; I want an open conversation about the charms of carnality…
I am declaring sexual freedom is not treason.
We can be all things consensually…
Wives, husbands, heauxs, asexual, pansexual, bisexual…
And yes we are more than that, but it's this world's erotic interests centering the proclivities we own.
Lives are not defined by a good bone, but we will excavate these freedoms beneath shame's stone.

I can't wait for the day to let out a free, Black moan.

DENNIS MAURICE

Deeply Hood

A Thought Addressed to Black Folk who have suffered with and because of the ingrained anti-Blackness.

BLACK WASHED | *A Collection of Essays, Poems, Dreams, and Letters Addressed to Black Folk*

Deeply Hood

I have been running on a track for decades.

Competitively I have won many races by proving I do not have one.

Blind of color and *hue*manity.

For years I have been in a race to prove that I am better than deeply hood niggas…

I keep running away and toward identities that I love but the world cannot.

I am a runner and a boxer.

Hitting you, but blacking my eye…

Refusing to see that I am bloody from holding broken glass mirrors that show a reflection I am ashamed of.

I keep fighting you…

I won; I hear applause.

I am a runner, a boxer, and a swimmer.

Backstroke, sidestroke, combat stroke, you name it, I will do it if it means you are out of this pool.

I am swimming laps around you just to say I swam laps around you.

My legs, arms, back, and body are worn and wilted…

I won; I hear applause.

Because I prefer chlorine filled pools with isolated sections to display your absence & my skill.

I am in a race to prove I do not have one.

Denying the heritage of our complexity because it will not fit into my code-switched identities.

I have been running, fighting, and swimming away from any association to deeply hood niggas.

Mocking the manner and voice used to passionately celebrate me, to cover up anti-Black insecurity.

And I am running away from the only folk at the finish line cheering for me.

HALOS & ~~Ten~~ HEADWRAPS

Black Washed is dedicated to my mother. The dedication I wrote to her welcomed you and as our final chapter's foreword author she will send you on your way. The title, Halos & Headwraps, came from my earliest memory. I woke up and I did not remember anything that happened prior—little glimmers, but I had no access to memory. At this time my grandma, mother, aunt, and I shared a bedroom in my grandparents' two-bedroom home. Oddly, I was not scared, because I knew I belonged there. I saw my grandma in a mint-colored nightgown with an ingeniously designed headwrap. I hopped over to her bed, from the twin-bed that my mother and I shared, because I knew I belonged to her in some way. I told her about my memory loss, and she listened and comforted me while weaving her arms securely behind my neck. I felt her warmth—I still feel it. A little later another woman with a genius headwrap came in and directed me to do crazy things like get in the shower. I knew it was wise to listen to her. She belonged there, too. I held her by the hip and before I could part my lips, my grandma told her about my apparent memory loss. She looked down at me and carefully wrapped her arms behind me and said, "I remember you." From that moment I knew how to identify safety. Now I reimagine headwraps as halos on the heads of angels who knew me when I did not know myself and held my neck safe with their wings.

Welcome to Chapter ten: Halos & Headwraps—Foreword Author: Adrianne S. Dumpson-Diggs.

BLACK WASHED | *A Collection of Essays, Poems, Dreams, and Letters Addressed to Black Folk*

Ten

Black Woman Foreword Author

Adrianne S. Dumpson-Diggs

Born in South Philadelphia, Adrianne S. Dumpson-Diggs is a Christian, mother, wife, and nonprofit leader. The mother of three men (Dennis, Devin, and Dylan), Adrianne is an alumnus of Lincoln University of Pennsylvania, the nation's first historically black college or university. In addition, she earned her master's degree in Human Services at 40 years old while raising children, being a wife, and working full-time.

With more than 25 years of experience in the non-profit sector, child welfare, and parent support services Adrianne is a seasoned veteran in the human & social services profession. In 1991 she founded the Parent Support Center, a holistic wellness incubator and community resource for single parents, women, and young families for 13 years. Today she leads a team of social service professionals for a large public assistance institution that provides necessary economic support to growing families in Pennsylvania.

Adrianne resides in the Western Suburbs of Philadelphia with her husband, Robert, and children. It is also worth mentioning that she is the mother of the author, Dennis Maurice. When she is not entertaining, renovating her home, or being a strong rock for family, she enjoys the practice of actualizing self-empowerment and exploring methods in spiritual wellness. She is also a YouTube creator & food influencer at **What Adrianne Thinks** (be sure to Like, Comment, and Subscribe).

BLACK WASHED | *A Collection of Essays, Poems, Dreams, and Letters Addressed to Black Folk*

We Must Clean Ourselves First

Adrianne S. Dumpson-Diggs

I used to tell people who were experiencing difficulties trying to repair people, situations, and/or general problems—"Yeah, I'm Florence Nightingale, too." I knew I could fix everyone—even those with extremely broken hearts, minds, and spiritual fortresses. Inwardly, I knew that all I was saying was, 'I am a flawed person attempting to fix others before reckoning with myself.'

We must clean ourselves first.

The concept of ensuring we care for *Self* before *Others* is something I learned while earning my master's degree in Human Services fifteen years ago. I am truly clear that you cannot do anything for anyone until you know about yourself and that was reinforced consistently for my classmates and I, a cohort of social service professionals, from day one at Lincoln University.

As students we were encouraged to share with transparency and my advisor told me to trust the process and the healing that can come from being a full participant. What I learned was life affirming. In the beginning, I had to quickly learn to trust while deciding how much to share, how deep to delve into my past, and how far to dream—in community—about my future.

One of our major assignment was to develop and discuss a timeline from Birth to age 72—the top of the timeline reflected our highs and the bottom related to our lows or difficult memories. I started by entering my birth date and then drew a line until I hit my first memory. My earliest memory was an Easter Sunday when I was about 3 years old and the family was capturing photos and then a few years later I remembered walking with my mother to meet my kindergarten teacher, Mrs. Robinson. I remember the latter because I was excited about going to school and that is the only memory I have of my mother as a noticeably young child. Then the bad memories take over, the death of my young cousin, the death of my mother's father, the Saturday ritual of getting my hair washed, straighten, and curled—*many a Black girl* know the was horror and weekly torture of a hot stove, straightening comb, sizzling grease, and a lot of "Gal, now I said keep ya ol' tender head still, ya hear!?!"

What I found interesting about this exercise was how easy I compiled unhappy or bad experiences, yet it was a chore to seek out happy memories as they seemed so distant, almost like they never happened. Although I knew that wasn't true, my lesson was that calling on hurt, for me, seemed easier to access—especially when you're amassed in hurt culturing. Hurt is a funny thing, because while it is built on disruption, it can be a comfortable place for many of us—especially when it's all you know. Developing this timeline forced me to seek joy and fight through the muck of my experiences to bring it out in my life. The Joys of an awesome mother and father, a dynamic family, friendship, and life extended for me to be able stand after the experience of pain, hurt, and disappointments.

BLACK WASHED | *A Collection of Essays, Poems, Dreams, and Letters Addressed to Black Folk*

Adlin Sinclair said "You are the embodiment of the information you choose to accept and act upon. To change your circumstances, you need to change your thinking and subsequent actions."

We must clean ourselves first.

My time at Lincoln and that quote by Sinclair guided me toward creating a spiritual place within myself that supported me in removing doubt and fear and intensifying my level of intention and gratitude. I am constantly learning how to be grateful for all things including the highs and lows in my life, because they have formed my character. I am grateful for all the things that make me, me.

I have learned a lot in my life and one thing is to wash my mind and spirit of negativity and the importance of protecting my heart from outside entities and sometimes from myself. Studying myself first, studying why I make choices, and being honest with me about me is my first act of cleansing—I own the right to clean me up first, before I let anyone else get in my water.

I am thankful for my strength holders in God, my mother, father, aunts, uncles, sisters, brothers, husband, and children, as they all play a part in shaping, guiding, and nurturing me to continue to grow into who I am and will be. However, they can only be guides for my journey and what more I become. All that is in store for us is guided by our spirit, our mission, and our drive. However, underneath it all, there is a desire to be clean and it's important, as Black women, that we are washed in knowing ourselves first. My journey and what I share with others is ultimately to find the courage to be honest with us about us. My dream is that we love ourselves so much, we remove the comfortable pillow of pain and get up fiercely with purpose— standing tall as Black women who know love so deeply that we cleaned ourselves first.

This is our water.

DENNIS MAURICE

How Is Sugar Born?

A Meditation Addressed to Black Transgender Folk

BLACK WASHED | *A Collection of Essays, Poems, Dreams, and Letters Addressed to Black Folk*

How Is Sugar Born?

"There are too many names of Black, Transgender (trans) folk who have been murdered. I wrote this meditative poem for my family. As we grieve the loss of Black trans minds, souls, beauty, and bodies let's remember that Black life does not start when hate kills us. How Is Sugar Born?"

One day I was thinking about sugar. How is sugar born? Like, where does it come from? No, I was not high… I was six.

I asked my grandma and she told me beautiful memories of sugar she ate off the cane. I remember her saying "Oh, that cane be so sweet!" Her memories were reaching out to her smile and showing off on her face and I saw how much she loved sweet sugar cane. But my question was still unanswered, "How is sugar born?"

From roots grow sweet cane near bayous, rivers, and lakes under hot beams of southern suns and daughters. Oh, that cane be so sweet. Sweet cane grows 20 feet high, clearly one of the closest farm stalks to heaven. 20 feet tall. Sweet & supple. Wrapped in a hard bamboo armor to protect all its authentic syrup. Oh, that cane be so sweet.

Its graceful leaves bend in the wind —just swishin'— you cannot miss that sweet cane… it welcomes you in. And even when you cut it down it grows back stronger and taller again. Strong stalks.

And those sugar cane leaves move like good weaves. Bouncing. Behaving. Misbehaving. Doing whatever they please. Oh, that cane be so sweet.

But the sad thing is that once that sweet cane is full grown, wild, and sturdy it gets chopped down. We remove all its sweetness and turn its diamond-colored blood into crystals for our coffee. Crystals for our cakes. Crystals for the Kool-Aid. And crystals in our Corn Flakes. Oh, that cane be so sweet.

Sturdy stalks that once held sacred saccharine syrups are chopped into bamboo earrings, tables, and chairs. And we never ask how the hell it got there.

We chew on its body until there is nothing left but straw. Then we spit it out after we have sucked the cane dry. I do not know how sugar is born, but this is how we allow sugar to die.

That cane be so sweet?

Where is sugar born?

And why do I only know how sugar dies?

Peace to all the Black trans queens, kings, and non-conforming royals.

***

Author's Note: While developing the content for *Black Washed*, I recognized that the thought leadership about Black Women can only be shared by Black Women. In turn, 10 Black Women supported it with their unique expressions as foreword authors. While it was not intentional to only include Black *cis-gender* women, I recognize the void of not having the fullest expression of Black Womanhood represented. Instead of tokening my community with an addition, I have chosen to move forward with greater purpose. My work applauds and celebrates the enduring beauty of Black life. There is more I can do to ensure that Black trans and non-binary folx are centered with amplified voices within my books and I promise you will see that in future publishing. I love you.

BLACK WASHED | *A Collection of Essays, Poems, Dreams, and Letters Addressed to Black Folk*

Optics & Capital

A Reflective Essay Addressed to Black Folk

DENNIS MAURICE

Optics & Capital

In January 2020, just before the deadliest global pandemic my generation has seen overwhelmed an exceedingly ill-equipped United States of America, I founded a consultancy and philanthropy whose mission is to amplify & invest in Black community genius in impactful ways. I believe deeply in Black folk as intelligent, critically thoughtful leaders and I needed to create space for us to empty our gifts as we define, in a world that we define. After 15 years as a nonprofit fundraiser and 36 years as a Black gay man, I have grown fatigued with how much, and the distances to which, government and profit maximizing institutions (particularly, but not limited to) will trek to manipulate and adulterate humanity. Parity, representation, access, and inclusion are fruitful for everyone, except the capitalist. In recognition, I decided to make our business my business and stay out of their business.

It is now June; and globally, a decision is made to play in the faces of Black folk… yet again. Breonna, Ahmaud, George, Tony, Riah, and countless others are killed by order of American principles and principalities and instead of honoring Black lives the choice is made to exploit Black death. The countless lives murdered by police and vigilantes, with no accountability, are vile disclosures of how much America is decried of humanity. Yet when warm-blooded Black lives were evacuated from narratives about our experiences to make room for the corporate branding centering our mortality we saw, firsthand, the *implication* that a Black death is the same as a Black nativity.

Adding greater depravity, the white-bending public sphere bastardized today's green book—also known as hashtags, created as a tool to guide us through a relentless horror story—to regenerate shareholder value amid financial crisis and reputation ruin. Black death was being used to garner cash and cachet. The murders of #AhmaudArbery, #RiahMilton, #GeorgeFloyd, #TonyMcDade, and #BreonnaTaylor consumed the lexicon and those of us alive in this skin were placed on hold until our hashtag is called.

In 2009, I published my first book, *What My Colored Eyes See*—inside lives a poem, "Target Practice," about the 2006 murder of Sean Bell & 1999 murder of Amadou Diallo.

I have been angry about this for years. This is not new.

This is America—a harbor for racism, patriarchy, and inequity. The more recent attacks on Black lives are appalling, yet America's heritage of hate for the living is equally as horrifying and corrupt.

As a pro-Black, gay man who is actively developing the capacity for anti-racism, I want, more than many things, to see an equitable, inclusive, accessible world that values every life.

BLACK WASHED | *A Collection of Essays, Poems, Dreams, and Letters Addressed to Black Folk*

As a pro-Black, gay man who is actively developing the capacity for anti-racism, I want, more than anything, to see the demise of white terrorism and its unrelenting legion.

Be clear: My work—in all its roots—embraces Black liberation and seeks to vitiate white terror and all its accomplices. I demand that same energy from others who claim they are not racist, xenophobic, misogynistic, anti-Black, ableist, capital-focused partners to white supremacy.

It is now July and optics have shifted. Aunt Jemima is out; Master bedrooms are no more; the Redskins are now the Washington Football Team; Uncle Ben ain't in charge of the rice; and a slew of other topical identities helped capital-focused partners to white supremacy find new ways to ensure shareholder value. However, Black life though visible is not an optic. We are proof of angels because of our ability to live no matter how many attempts to kill us. We are also living, breathing, active people whose lives do not begin when we die. Yet, in this country our lives are not considered; instead, the ways in which our lives are taken are often the leading narratives.

It's August and my business is alive with organizations clamoring for support of their "diversity, equity, and inclusion efforts." One day while researching through a swath of white data I counted 14 data points about the Black experience that shared a different way we are killed—economically, physically, mentally, by police, by each other, through policy, through fatness, via queerness, because of womanhood, because of manhood, because of childhood, in the womb, through sex, and Covid-19. No data point in this comprehensive survey asked or addressed Black life without the fetishization of Black mortality. But those are the optics. Black life is not valuable in its calmness within this constructed reality. In America's milieu, our stories must be mused through fatal conflicts and debilitating, hard-to-digest existences that disavow Black folk from having a robust and humane life. As such when non-Black people, entities, and things advocate for Black folk it is generally void of any acknowledgement of Black life.

It is September, and without boasting, I am in higher demand. Companies all over the country want the *race folk* to help them through these trying times. Requests for me to help whiteness make sense of whiteness are plentiful—I deny most. I am asked to be paid to create plans, statements, workshops, and strategies and in turn companies will decide, without me, how it fits in their enterprise-wide strategies. These are the optics. Philanthropists are giving one-time gifts to Black, Indigenous, and People of Color centered initiatives and after cutting checks will soon become unreachable for future investments. Optics are leading again.

And here lies the problem, we continue to perform as if this country has reason to be humane, empathetic, and radical in its voyage to understand why America is America. We know that America is considered great by some and many because of its ability to pillage the non-Westernized world for power and privilege and in turn create a viable value proposition centering its superiority. Anything, anyone centered in an American sensibility has no skill, motivation, or benefit in believing in a diverse, equitable, inclusive, and accessible landscape for any folk disregarded by this place.

Personally, I have higher tolerance, than I desire, for mediocrity and low bar for expecting authenticity from whiteness and its investors. Therefore, my expectations for their respect of life is so low that, to some extent, name changes and brand repairs feel like progress. They are not. They only keep the truth about this state-of-being topical, at best, and financially solvent, in perpetuity.

Money and fake love are the root, not the remedy. Our leverage is our resilience <u>and</u> ability to uproot mirrors from *this side of soil* that reveal the things that we will never forget.

Black life is a carnival and a sanctuary showcasing our journeys with joy and pain through eras of blood-stained glass. It is now December, and eyes are closed, but no one is sleep.

Everyone is awake.

OUR FINAL SUBMISSION

Alive In This Skin

A Poem Addressed to Black Folk

Alive In This Skin

If I'm being honest
It is an infuriating torment to see… to hear…
grown white bodies and minds emote
The stress of realizing how racist America is…

I was introduced to racism
As a Black boy
In Philadelphia.

I was introduced to anti-Blackness
As a young professional
In well-meaning nonprofits, liberal government, and within philanthropy.

Being Black I learned,
Well before COVID-19,
How important it is to wear a mask
For my safety and survival.

Since childhood I have had to navigate…
Explicit forms of hate…
And for nearly 40 years I have had to choose between…
The hazard of disinfecting this hostile virus or the complicated joy of living a little while longer.

My understandings of race, racism, bias, anti-Blackness, prejudice, whiteness, white terror, hate, and injustice were not revealed on May 25, 2020; May 27, 2020; March 13, 2020; July 13, 2015; or even November 25, 2006.

I have lived with what America and her white children choose to grapple with today for my entire life. You may see us grotesquely folded and drained of our rich, warm blood as it stolen by the concrete, but we live, too.

Death did not raise us.

We are alive in this skin.

THE FASTENING

Epilogue

Since I began writing my first book, *What My Colored Eyes See: The Words of a Decorated Child*, in 2004, I have been crafting essays, poems, dreams, and letters addressed to Black folk. That collection, which exists in part on these pages, has been supported by the elegance of Black women foreword authors who generously lent their brilliance. I am grateful that one-third of *Black Washed* has been confidently curated by Black women; especially the women that pushed my spine straight when I slouched on my gifts.

I thought I completed our manuscript for *Black Washed* in 2017. I dug deep for the right language and I was completing my final read of that version of *Black Washed* when I was gut punched. What I read showed me pandering to my folk and it caused me to question one of the things I know is my gift. I was laying deep in a bloated mess of rhyming words and parody and had to find my way out. My authenticity saved me. It was the repellent for my own bullshit.

"If you want to fly, you got to give up the shit that weighs you down."
- Toni Morrison
(Song of Solomon, 1977)

Once the bind on my true heart was released, I had room to publish this version of *Black Washed*. I am proud that what you have read is more than regurgitation of thoughts about this world held hostage. This is an intimate anthology honoring our heritage and ability to reveal and passionately articulate the truth.

I feel most comfortable with Black folk and I have spent more than two decades writing poetry, essays, letters, reflections, dreams, and ideas guided by our light. I hope this thread translates my embrace of our knotted experiences as I intended. I hope you feel loved and cared for in ways that feel familiar & fresh.

Black Washed is a love letter, a sharp read, a du-rag, a headwrap, or a silk bonnet, a group chat, and an earnest "Good morning, Beautiful." text from me to Black folk everywhere. Black lives are made of matter and we are designed to take up space. As I have admired through eloquent articulations of elders and contemporaries like Morrison, Baldwin, Lorde, Clifton, Blow, Gay, Coates, Gregory, Muhammad *(Abdul-Aliy)*, Simone, hooks, Mock, Hemphill, Hughes, brown *(adrienne maree)*, Shange, and Sapphire, I want to create space for breathing Black worlds. Black worlds that embrace our complex existence in silos we build, own, and relish. We exist outside of, absent of, and relieved of white domains and *Black Washed* is my chance to be one of many that have and will continue to investigate and reveal the grandeur in Black worlds.

THE FASTENING

I grew up in the Black church. If you did as well you will understand these analogies: My first book, *What My Colored Eyes See: The Words of a Decorated Child*, is kin to Sunday morning service. *Black Washed* is the break before second service—the fried chicken, cake, and church punch to hold you over. *Black Washed* spans generations and sensibilities and admires the sanctuaries we build between our hands and the miry clay.

I hope this sparks discussion as a revelation that Black life is an environment, in and to itself, absent of white things, and marked by love.

Black life is a carnival and a sanctuary showcasing our journeys with joy and pain through eras of blood-stained glass. And that alone is worthy of celebrations.

Black folk are filled with incendiaries. We are the fuse. We are the match. We got the fire. We are the bomb.

With Fire Filled Love,

WE CREATE THE JOY

"…and that alone is worthy of celebrations."
-Dennis Maurice

***

THE FASTENING

Tunaunda Furaha.

(We create the joy.)

WE CREATE THE JOY

THIS BOOK SUPPORTS THE BLACK ECONOMY IN SALES & PROCUREMENT

This is self-published and financed through the author's publishing company, VeryBlackBooks.com, via a print-on-demand portal. The author receives 100% of <u>profits</u> when books are purchased directly from Very Black Books.

Moreover, 100% of the services & expertise used to produce the book's content were provided by Black people & businesses that were paid at market rate or better.

As long as there are Black folk, we will strive for this standard of excellence. Thank you!

- Dennis Maurice

FOR MORE INFORMATION ON *BLACK WASHED* OR DENNIS MAURICE VISIT:

www.iamDennisMaurice.com | www.InvestBLK.org | www.VeryBlackBooks.com

@DennisMaurice | @VeryBlackBooks

www.ingramcontent.com/pod-product-compliance
Lightning Source LLC
Chambersburg PA
CBHW041410300426
44114CB00028B/2976